Highland Hermit

The Remarkable Life
of James McRory Smith

By James Carron

PUBLISHING

Amenta Publishing

www.amentapublishing.co.uk

Highland Hermit

The Remarkable Life of James McRory Smith

By James Carron

First published 2010 by Amenta Publishing

This edition published 2012

Copyright © James Carron 2012

1

I only met James McRory Smith once. It was a meeting in the loosest sense of the word. Between us stood an old wooden door, the latch firmly down, barring entry to the tumbledown cottage he called home. There was no face-to-face contact, no pleasantries swapped, just anonymous confrontation.

On one side of the warped, weather-beaten boards slumped two exhausted hillwalkers seeking refuge, an escape from the hostile elements in the only building for miles around. On the other, there was an angry old man unwilling to surrender his privacy. I remember the moment well. It was late summer, 1992. And it was late at night.

A friend – David – and I set off earlier in the day with the intention of walking from Durness to Sandwood Bay where we planned to pitch our tent in the dunes before hiking back through the hills to Durness. The weather was good as we set off and after crossing the Kyle of Durness on the tiny ferryboat that flits back and forth over this narrow channel during the summer months, we shouldered our heavy packs and headed off along the surfaced track leading ultimately to the lighthouse at Cape Wrath.

A minibus conveys tourists back and forth across this wild and uninhabited country. But we chose to walk, making the most of our short time on the Parph. The road climbs steeply from the ferryman's cottage, heading north above the shoreline to the old crofts at Achiemore and Daill. Here the route leaves the Kyle and its glorious beaches of golden sand and heads west over a vacant landscape of heather moor concealing little more than a spattering of small lochans and the occasional empty cottage, abandoned to the elements.

With the dust slowly settling behind the departing tourist minibus, we marched into the unknown. Our only guide was the thin strip of potholed tarmac originally constructed in the early 19th century to serve the lighthouse. Prior to the Second World War there was a thriving community living on the Parph. In the 1930s, 35 people lived and worked the land west of the Kyle of Durness. The men were shepherds, employed by two local farms to tend the flocks, and their children attended a small school, once the most remote on the British mainland.

James McRory Smith – Howard Patrick

In addition to servicing the lighthouse, the road was a vital lifeline for these secluded families. A weekly lorry run, taking food, fuel and other essentials to the lighthouse keepers dropped off supplies at cottages and crofts along the way. The Durness-based postman who would cycle out with the mail also used the road, three times a week. Now the only regular traffic is the tourist minibus, which we watched fade into the distance.

As we tramped on, the fine weather that encouraged us to don our boots after breakfast was rapidly deteriorating. Banks of dark cloud lumbered in from the sea and after a preliminary smattering of light drizzle they mustered sufficient vigour to send in a full-blown rainstorm.

As much by good fortune as by good meteorological planning, we stumbled upon a derelict cottage at Inshore. Although dilapidated, it still boasted most of its roof and that was enough for us. We snuck in through an open window and shook off the worst of the rain.

Inside, we settled down to make a brew, hoping the weather would pass and allow us to continue on our journey unhindered. We were clearly not the first people to have sought refuge here. Strewn across the floor were the remnants of military ration packs left by soldiers who regularly visit Cape Wrath and the Parph for training exercises.

Anyone who has ever cast an eye over the Ordnance Survey map for this far-flung corner of Scotland will not have failed to notice, emblazoned in bold pink lettering, the words 'Danger Area'. Thanks to its remote location and absence of a resident population, Cape Wrath has long been used for army, navy and air force activities, involving both our own forces and those from other NATO countries.

The so-called 'Danger Area' starts just west of the Kyle of Durness and extends towards the bay at Kervaig and inland to Loch Airigh na Beinne and Loch na Gainmhich. Army exercises regularly take place on the land, while tiny islands – some no bigger than rocks or sea stacks – are subjected to aerial bombardment. For this reason alone, it is probably fair to say this is one of the least visited parts of Britain.

We had, however, decided to visit and after downing our tea, we set off again, wandering out into the last vestiges of the rainstorm. We made good progress and by late afternoon reached Cape Wrath, the most northwesterly tip of the British mainland, and its lighthouse. Built in 1828 by Robert Stevenson using granite quarried at nearby Clash Carnoch, the tower is 20-metres high and stands right on the edge of a sheer cliff that plunges over 120 metres down into the swirling froth of the Atlantic Ocean. A little to the east of the lighthouse, the highest sea cliffs in mainland Britain are to be found.

Prior to the lighthouse's construction, the cape was a notorious danger point for vessels attempting to enter or leave the Pentland

Firth. A crew of six men lived and worked here, operating the light and maintaining the complex. Although accessible by road, some supplies came by sea, with an annual visit by the lighthouse tender vessel, which brought diesel and paraffin oil. The site was manned until March 31, 1998, when the light was automated. It is now remotely monitored from the Northern Lighthouse Board's offices in Edinburgh.

In 1930, the men stationed at the lighthouse were joined on the cape by the staff of a signal station, constructed by the shipping insurance giant Lloyds of London on a low hill to the south of the complex to keep an eye on shipping. It now lies in ruins while the lighthouse continues to offer a beacon to passing ships.

Our journey took us south from the lighthouse. We were forced to relinquish the security of the single-track road and find our own way across pathless moor. We set a course inland, away from the coastal cliffs. Visibility was good. We knew time was not on our side, but we were prepared to cover the final miles to Sandwood Bay by torchlight if necessary. The going, however, was not so good. The ground beneath our feet rose and fell incessantly. We ducked in and out of gullies, hopped back and forth across streams, fought ankle-trapping heather and squelched anxiously around increasingly expansive – and increasingly moist – mires of marsh and bog.

Progress was slow and the last vestiges of energy soon ebbed from our aching legs. Occasionally we stumbled upon what looked to be a path and spirits soared, only to be dashed when we discovered it was just a short-lived sheep or deer track. With the light fading, we contemplated pitching our tent, but forays for potential campsites in the thick heather were fruitless. So we dug out our torches, set a compass bearing and pressed on, battling to hold a straight line over the topsy-turvy terrain.

We were exhausted and every step forward was a struggle. Tempers quickly frayed. There were arguments about the accuracy of the compass bearing, where exactly we were and why we were not progressing as planned. There were no landmarks to judge our progress by, no visible points of reference we could relate our map to. If ever there was a time to pull together, this was it. But we were drifting apart. Conversation ceased and we plodded on in silence. Sandwood Bay seemed more distant than ever.

But at least it wasn't raining. There was some small comfort in that fact. We may have been wandering around in the darkness, unsure of where we were and, in these pre-GPS days, with all our hopes pinned on a small plastic device with a wobbly red needle, but at least we were warm and dry. Sadly, however, that was not too last much longer. For the second time that day, a squall of light drizzle heralded the arrival of a rather more robust drenching. The heavens opened, battering us with a potent cocktail of rain and wind. We pulled on waterproof jackets and over-trousers, determined we would not be beaten. But it was devilishly wet and cold. All we could hope for was that the next rise we mounted would reveal Sandwood Bay in all its glory.

Of course, it didn't. All that happened was the rain continued to fall, the wind continued to whistle and we continued to walk. We were locked into a vicious cycle of hope followed by despair. Then, to our utter astonishment, we spotted a small wisp of smoke rising into the black night sky.

Strathchailleach – James Carron

It was so very faint, but it stopped us dead in our tracks. We turned to face one another, seeking confirmation. Did we see smoke, or were we hallucinating? Anxiously we turned our heads and focussed our tired eyes on the horizon ahead. Yes, there was definitely smoke.

With trembling fingers, we consulted our map, scanning the grid squares by torchlight for any mark of habitation. There was a tiny square accompanied by the word 'Strathchailleach'. Spirits lifted, we lurched forward with renewed fervour, witnessing a spring in our step that had, up until that point, been sadly lacking. A tiny cottage came into view. It was a squat little structure, hugging the ground in the base of the valley below us. There was no light emanating from it, only the steady funnelling of grey smoke. It was an oasis in our desert.

In a second all the pain, anguish and frustration of the night vanished. We walked, jogged and then ran, tearing through the wiry heather towards the little house. One final obstacle presented itself – a fast flowing little river, its current swelled by the night's rain. But we splashed through the water without a second thought and arrived below the smoking chimney.

We rounded the cottage, passing a dim glow of light struggling to escape from a diminutive window, and paused briefly to catch our breath by the front door. It was an old wooden door, flecked with shards of peeling paint and framed by blocks of lichen-encrusted stone. David lifted a hand to the latch and gently depressed it. He pushed the door, but it failed to yield. It was locked. Our hearts fell in unison.

'What now?' David asked, his voice barely audible above the wind.

'Knock,' I suggested.

So he did, a light tap at first.

Nothing.

He rapped his knuckles across the wood again, this time more forcefully.

From the bowels of the cottage we heard a loud, almost animal-like roar erupt. Shaken, we took a step back. There was no evidence to suggest this was someone's home – no car or Land Rover parked up outside. There were no power or telephone cables connected to the cottage. No one could possibly live here beneath the rusty corrugated iron roof, or so we thought.

We were cold, tired and hungry. We knocked again and drew an instant response – angry shouting and swearing. Anxiously we waited to see if the door would open. Would we find ourselves starring down the barrels of a loaded shotgun when all we sought was shelter from the elements?

The tirade of verbal abuse subsided almost as quickly as it had erupted. The door, for its part, stayed firmly shut.

Reluctantly we decided to leave, but before we stepped back into the night, I pressed my face up against the front window from which the light was coming. It was difficult to see much. The pains of glass were small, grubby and encrusted with cobwebs. The room beyond was terribly gloomy.

From within, two beady eyes, framed by a flat cap and a rambling white beard, starred back at me. There was a man in there, and he had an axe in his hand.

Sandwood Bay – James Carron

I recoiled from the window, grabbed David's arm and yanked him away from the cottage. We sloshed through reedy marsh, snagging our waterproof trousers on rusty fence wire, before finally hitting solid ground. We walked on, faster than we had done all day. And we didn't look back until we were well clear of the cottage.

A vague path led us up to Lochan nan Sac and from there we descended to Sandwood Bay. We pitched our tent in the lea of a sand dune and collapsed into our sleeping bags. Before I zipped up the tent door, I took one last look at the ridge above us, squinting through the darkness to see if an angry old man with beady eyes and an axe had pursued us. Thankfully, the coast was clear.

It was noon before we rose the next day. Over breakfast I told David what I had seen through the window. He was alarmed and thankful I had not shared this information with him while we were still out on the moor in the dead of the night. For my part, the fear of what I witnessed subsided in my sleep and I felt a little foolish that I had gone to the extent of checking the ridge before bedding down.

We continued on our way, spending our second night out at Strathan bothy, in Strath Shinary. Unlike Strathchailleach, we found the door open and had the place to ourselves. We endured a cold night on a hard floor after all attempts to find something to burn in the grate proved futile.

The following morning, stiff as boards, we hiked up to the col at the top of the glen and descended to the road, tramping tarmac back to Durness. It was a memorable hike, for many reasons. The one, however, that stuck in my mind was our brief visit to Strathchailleach and the welcome, or rather lack of, that we encountered there. I found it hard to fathom that someone lived there. But the reaction of the occupant and the vehement opposition to our arrival suggested a very protective attitude to the property. It felt as if we were trying to break into someone's home and they were protecting their little place on this earth come what may.

Back home, the matter briefly rested, occasionally airing itself over a pint with David in the pub, or over a whisky by the fire at another bothy. Then, a few months after our expedition to Sandwood Bay,

Strathchailleach came to the fore again. The question playing on my mind was finally answered.

On Sunday, October 11, I settled down to read the day's newspapers. As I opened my copy of the *Sunday Mail*, I immediately spotted a familiar face. Starring out at me from page three, under the headline 'Take a Hike Jimmy!' was James McRory Smith, billed in the accompanying text as Scotland's hardiest pensioner. Here was the man with the beady eyes and the axe who met my curious gaze on that stormy night at Strathchailleach.

The story confirmed that he did indeed live as a recluse in the former shepherd's cottage. The piece concentrated mainly on the lengthy trek James undertook each week to pick up his pension and provisions. He made a round trip of 26 miles, walking out to the Post Office at Balchrick and then heading down the single-track road to Kinlochbervie.

We knew from our own experience that Strathchailleach was not an easy place to reach. Approaching from the north, we spent many hours seeking the cottage out.

James McRory Smith – Sunday Mail

From the south, the journey is slightly less complex. A track that ultimately degenerates into a rough and ready path runs from Blairmore, on he road between Kinlochbervie and Sheigra, to Sandwood Bay. From there, a route must be carefully picked over open hillside. Historically, there was a pony track to Strathchailleach, but over time this was erased by the encroachment of heather, grass and marsh.

James' home was indeed remote. It was quite possibly the most remote dwelling on the British mainland and it is fair to say it was the last occupied primitive house in Scotland. There was no mains water, no electricity and no telephone line. So why did he choose to live there, facing such hardship?

There is little doubt that his key reason for settling at Strathchailleach was the solitude afforded by such a secluded spot. Prior to his arrival he spent many years on the road, moving from one labouring job to another and wandering from one part of Scotland to another. He never settled in one place for any length of time. He made no contact with his family and had no close friends. He slept out under the stars and briefly occupied other abandoned dwellings. Indeed, immediately prior to his arrival at Strathchailleach, he spent some time living in one of the abandoned cottages on the Parph we had passed on our walk from the Kyle of Durness to Cape Wrath.

He was frequently referred to as a hermit, both by people who knew him in Kinlochbervie and in occasional articles written about him over the years. The *Oxford English Dictionary* defines a hermit as a 'person living in solitude as a religious discipline' or 'a reclusive or solitary person'. The word hermit comes from the Greek term 'eremos', meaning 'solitary'.

James – who was often referred to as Sandy – was a solitary man, there is no doubt about that, and he led a reclusive lifestyle. However, there is no evidence to suggest religion played any part in this decision. Although born into a Roman Catholic family, he was not a regular churchgoer and some of his activities over the years were decidedly unholy.

He arrived at Strathchailleach in the early 1960s and lived at the bothy for over three decades, reluctantly vacating the cottage in 1994 when old age and ill-health forced him back into society. His life at Strathchailleach was a simple one, free of the stresses and strains most of us face on a day-to-day basis. He may not have had the luxury of piped water, gas or electricity, but at the same time he did not have to worry about finding the money to pay a mortgage, rent or utility bills. A modest income enabled him to buy food, drink and cigarettes and the surrounding land endowed him with a steady supply of fish, game, firewood and peat.

There was no need for James to get up in the morning to go to work in a factory or office. He was free of the daily grind many of us face. That is not to say he was an idle man. His priorities were just different. He worked hard simply to survive, completing a backbreaking round of daily chores, such as fetching water, cutting peat or gathering driftwood from the coastline and hauling it home across the moor.

James' way of life belonged to a bygone era. His simple existence was more akin to the 19th century crofters who occupied the land before him. In the outside world consumerism was becoming increasingly rife. Disposable incomes were higher than at any point in history and people were spending increasing amounts of their money on their homes, filling them with the latest electrical and electronic equipment, making their lives easier and more comfortable.

Yet James had no interest in such modern indulgences. The only piece of electrical equipment he owned was a small battery-powered radio. There was no cooker – not even a simple gas stove – at Strathchailleach. He cooked his meals over an open fire and in place of a fridge he stored his perishables in the cool water of a nearby lochan. He never owned a television set, a DVD player or a computer. The only luxuries in his life were whisky, cigarettes, magazines and books, most of which had been discarded by others.

Living alone, James did not have to tailor his plans around family members or friends. Although a reclusive character, he did not shun human company entirely. Some visitors to the bothy remember him as a genial host, enjoying long conversations over a cup of tea or a dram or two of whisky. He interacted with the people of Kinlochbervie and the neighbouring crofting townships and there were friends in the community, people who looked out for him. However, dealings with others tended to be forged on James' own terms and he lived free of the complexities of a close emotional or physical relationship. There is strong evidence to suggest this is one of the main reasons why he opted to change his life so dramatically.

Delving into his background, it is clear that two of the most significant, life-changing decisions he ever made related to women he was close to. The first involved his mother and the second his wife. It was the latter that set him on the path to Strathchailleach and his life as a recluse.

James' frugality could hold a lesson for us all. Although it was never his intention to demonstrate an alternative path – he took little interest in what others thought of his lifestyle choices – his simple existence at Strathchailleach shows that human beings can exist, even in this modern age, with few material possessions. At a time when there is increasing concern over our impact on the planet and its finite resources, we could do worse than take a leaf out of his book.

Living without a car, electricity and many of the consumer goods we all take for granted, his carbon footprint was negligible. Although his possessions were few, he made the most of what he did have, creating very little waste. There was nothing in his life that he did not need. Everything he owned was essential to his survival and others left much of it in their wake, from the discarded books he read and re-read to the salvaged wooden fish and fruit boxes he fashioned into furniture. He had no need for a gym membership – walking kept him healthy to the extent that he never once called on the services of a doctor during his time at Strathchailleach.

It is perhaps an extreme example of an environmentally friendly existence, but James was content with it, describing his life as 'perfect'. How many of us can truly say that about our own lives?

*****

14

2

James McRory Smith spent over half his life as a recluse, wandering at will from one place to the next until he settled at Strathchailleach. His childhood, however, contrasted sharply with this solitary lifestyle. But there were early clues to the path he would eventually follow.

At 6.30am on March 6, 1925, James was born into a large Roman Catholic family in the ancient burgh of Dumbarton. Already there were six older siblings in the brood – Andrew, Bill, Rita, Nell, Frank and Davy and over subsequent years younger brothers and sisters were to follow – Winnie, Lilly, Lisbeth, John, twins Bobby and June, Sheila and, the youngest, Thomas. There was another sister too, Agnes, but she died in infancy.

In all, 15 children occupied the family home at Sandpoint, a spit of land wedged between the River Clyde and the River Leven. And the house they lived in was by no means large. It was a simple three-bedroom flat, one of four in a block sitting in the shadow of the burgeoning Clyde shipbuilding industry.

His father Andrew Smith was a riveter to trade, working for William Denny & Brothers, the town's largest employers. His mother Elizabeth (nee McRory) looked after the home and brought the children up. Both Andrew and Elizabeth were born and bred in Dumbarton. They married on April 6, 1914, at Blythwood, Glasgow, and set up home at Sandpoint, where the majority of the men worked at the Denny yard.

Money was tight and discipline was strict. But it was a happy and loving home environment in which James grew up.

'We were a large family.' his sister Winnie recalled. 'The house we lived in was not big so it was difficult to get any time to yourself. There never seemed to be a minute's peace as there was always something going on. And over the years there were more and more people about as nieces and nephews visited.

'I remember there were just three bedrooms but one of them was only a small box room so we spent a lot of our time outside, playing in the street or down by the river.

'Mum spent all her time looking after us. It was a big job, cooking and cleaning and doing all the washing. Everything happened in the kitchen. It was always busy in there.

'Dad worked at Denny's and I remember we would often go down to see him, taking a ginger bottle with tea in it for his break. Mum always wrapped it in a jersey to keep the tea warm.

'There was never much money but we got by. At Christmas dad carved dolls from pegs for the girls and we got an orange and an apple each and colouring books. We were happy with these simple presents,' she added.

Andrew Smith worked hard to support his family. William Denny & Brothers was, by the 1930s, the leading shipbuilder in Dumbarton, although the firm's roots can be traced back to 1814 when founder William Denny began building steamships on the banks of the River Clyde at Dumbarton. Following his death, three of his sons set up a company of marine architects, Denny Brothers, in 1844 to design steamers.

They leased Kirk Yard, on the banks of the River Leven, and, a year later, took over Wood Yard, the premises formerly occupied by their late father's business at Sandpoint. With an initial workforce of just 14 men, the operation quickly prospered and in 1849 William Denny & Brothers was formed. In those early days every aspect of shipbuilding took place on the Clyde, from design through the forging of iron to the construction of the final vessel. There were jobs for local men and an influx of workers from across Scotland and Ireland.

With healthy order books, the company expanded rapidly, acquiring the North Yard, on the River Leven, and enlarging its engineering workshops. In 1867, a new purpose-built yard opened on the River Leven and the arrival of William Denny, grandson of the founder, brought new blood and innovation. A skilled scientist, he pioneered radical technology and methods and was responsible for the creation of the Denny Ship Model Experiment Tank, a ground-breaking test facility that allowed the company to evaluate fresh hull designs in wax model form. Created in 1882 and stretching the length of a football pitch, it was the first commercial ship model testing tank in the world and continues in use to this day.

William Denny & Brothers continued to grow, amalgamating its own businesses and swallowing up smaller yards. At the start of the 20th century, the company was constructing ships of all types for operators around the world. In 1901, it completed the King Edward, the world's first passenger turbine steamer.

The First World War brought steel shortages and a dip in the shipbuilding market due to over-capacity, but the 1920s saw prosperity return with the company continuing to reap rich rewards from its reputation for research and innovation, particularly in the development of high-pressure turbines that afforded greater speed.

With a growing young family, Andrew Smith was never short of work with a firm often described as one of the most prolific shipbuilders in the world. Young James was raised in a thriving and, thanks to the arrival of navvies from Ireland, increasingly diverse community. It was also a community proud of its historic links, and this would not have been lost on James who, according to his family, always took a keen interest in his surroundings.

One of the most dominant features of the local landscape is Dumbarton Rock – known by locals simply as the Rock – on which sits Dumbarton Castle, a legendary stronghold described by King Henry VIII as the key to the realm. Standing guard over the Firth of Clyde, the twin-pronged volcanic plug lies just across the River Leven from the site of what was then the Smith family home at Sandpoint and could not have failed to capture James' imagination.

For many local youngsters the Rock itself was a stronger draw than the historic castle perched atop the steep volcanic slopes. The cliffs and crags and the giant boulders at their base offered an exciting outdoor adventure playground for Dumbarton's youth.

But play was only a part of life for the children of Dumbarton. There was education too and James, like his brothers and sisters, attended St Patrick's School (now Our Lady & St Patrick's High School), a short walk from the family home. Boys and girls both attended junior school there but the senior years were separated, boys moving upstairs at St Patrick's while girls transferred to another building, called Notre Dam.

At school, James' light coloured hair earned him the nickname 'Smudge'. An intelligent child, he was more gifted artistically than academically. He was keen on drawing and painting and took an interest in the wildlife and countryside around Dumbarton.

His sister Winnie said, 'James was very artistic. He was always drawing pictures, even as a wee boy. My dad was like that too. He used to do some beautiful drawings. I think there must have been a real artistic streak running through the family.'

Art was an interest James pursued throughout his life, both during his years on the road and when he finally settled at Strathchailleach. However, as a boy he could not have known where he would ultimately end up, but according to his family there were some early pointers to the life of solitude he latterly craved.

'James always was a bit of a loner, even as a boy,' Winnie continued. 'He was a deep, self-contained person. He was like dad in that respect. They both had great strength of character and were very self-reliant. Maybe it was because James had grown up in a big family where it was very difficult to find peace and quiet. Maybe that was what he was looking for.'

For James and his brothers a career in the Clyde shipyards awaited when they left full time education. In the 1930s, when James was in his teens, the Denny yard had a healthy order book and there were plenty of other yards on the river looking for workers to meet the demand for new ships.

The future looked bright and James may very well have followed in his father's footsteps, embarking upon an apprenticeship and learning a trade. But then his mother died and the world as he knew it changed forever.

Elizabeth Smith was in her 50th year when she passed away. James was just 17. There was no illness, no warning that something was wrong.

'In the end I think she was just worn out,' Winnie said. 'She brought up a large family and it was very hard work for her.'

The death of Elizabeth was a major turning point for James, who, of all the children, was probably closest to his mother.

'I think mum's death hit James hard. He left home a short time after the funeral and it was a few years before he was seen again,' Winnie added.

Rather than enter the shipyards, James enlisted with the army.

In 1942, Britain was at war with Germany. With his beloved mother laid to rest, 17-year-old James left home and joined the army, following in the footsteps of his older brothers who entered military service, both with the British Army and Royal Navy. There was a proud military tradition in the family; Lance Corporal David McRory and Private William McRory both fought and died in the First World War. The two men received the Military Medal and their sacrifice is commemorated on Dumbarton's War Memorial, in the town's Levengrove Park.

Precise information on James' military service is scarce as official records for World War Two service personnel have not been made public and the records that do exist can only be released to close family. Unfortunately, they are not in possession of the information required to unlock these files.

Occasional references and anecdotal information suggest James served with the Black Watch Regiment. A *Sunday Mail* report on his life at Strathchailleach, published in 1992, refers to him as an 'ex-Black Watch soldier'. However, the regimental museum and archive at Balhousie Castle, in Perth, has been unable to confirm whether or not this was the case and contact with veterans has failed to unearth any recollections of a young soldier called James McRory Smith.

His sister Winnie's initial memory is that James enlisted with the Argyll & Sutherland Highlanders and this is a position supported by the fact that Dumbarton lies within the regiment's traditional recruiting ground.

Whichever regiment he joined, it is certain, given the date James enlisted, that he served with the 51st (Highland) Infantry Division.

The division incorporated, within the 153rd Infantry Brigade, the 5th Battalion Black Watch and, within the 154th Infantry Brigade, the 1st and 7th Battalions of the Black Watch and the 7th Battalion Argyll & Sutherland Highlanders.

The 51st (Highland) Infantry Division began life in 1920 as part of the Territorial Army. In 1939, it was sent to France, joining the British Expeditionary Force where soldiers of the 51st, under the command of the French Army, patrolled a section of the Maignot Line at Metz. In May 1940, the line came under sustained attack from the Germans and the division was forced to pull back. Efforts were made to withdraw the soldiers but on June 12 the 51st was forced to surrender.

All was not, however, lost. Back in Scotland, a new 51st (Highland) Infantry Division was created from the 9th (Highland) Infantry Division and, after training, it was sent to Aldershot in 1942 in preparation for a return to battle. It is this division that James most likely served with.

From Aldershot, the division was sent to North Africa where it came under the command of General Montgomery's 8th Army. Initially based in Egypt, the 51st fought in the Battle of El Alamein, assisting in the key campaign to drive German and Italian troops out of North Africa.

It is not know whether James fought in North Africa. His family believe his wartime activities were confined to Europe, so while he may not have seen service in Africa there is a good chance he was with the 51st when it moved to Sicily in 1943, joining an allied invasion force that took and held the Italian island.

The division returned to Britain having sustained over 6700 casualties in North Africa and Sicily. Leave, however, was brief and, in June 1944, the 51st was back in action as part of the invasion of Normandy. A number of units landed on the French coast on D-Day and others followed over subsequent days.

From a beachhead near Caen, the 51st pushed on to defeat German troops at Falaise and St Valery-en-Caux, the town where the original 51st (Highland) Infantry Division was forced to surrender in 1940. It was a particularly sweet and celebrated victory.

Battles followed at Le Havre, Calais and Dunkirk as the division moved east into Belgium and Holland, securing strategic ports for allied shipping and creating a safe corridor for troop movements through northern Europe.

In February 1945, the 51st was approaching Germany, spearheading the 1st Canadian Army's assault on the Rhineland. On March 23, the division's soldiers set out to establish a bridgehead over the Rhine at Rees and despite two days of heavy and sustained enemy attack this was successfully achieved.

After a brief period of rest, the division started to advance into northern Germany, pushing from Rees up to Bremen. On May 8, 1945, German forces finally surrendered and the 51st (Highland) Infantry Division marched into Berlin. In November 1945, the pipes and drums of the division celebrated victory with a parade in the fallen city's Olympic Stadium.

The arrival of the division in Berlin ties in with anecdotal evidence that placed James in the city at the end of the war. As a member of the 51st (Highland) Infantry Division, he would have witnessed – and played his part – in much bloody conflict in northern Europe. Battles at Goch and Rees were particularly intense and come VE-Day, the division had sustained over 15,000 casualties. For his part, James survived without any significant injury and evaded capture, unlike his brother Bill, who also fought during the Second World War and was held for many months as a prisoner of war in Japan.

With war over, the 51st (Highland) Infantry Division remained in Germany for a year on occupational duties. James returned to Scotland and made brief contact with his family in Dumbarton before taking work as a scaffolding erector in Glasgow. However, he didn't settle and a short time later he re-enlisted and returned to Germany.

James would have found a country struggling to recover from the aftermath of war. Concerted allied bombings left cities, industry and infrastructure in ruin. Thousands of people were homeless and hungry and there was a huge influx of refugees from the east.

In August 1945, pending a peace treaty, the occupying forces – Britain, France, America and the Soviet Union – divided the country into four military zones. Britain took charge of the north – the heavily industrialised Ruhr valley, the North Sea coast and the key cities of Cologne, Dortmund, Dusseldorf, Hamburg, Bremen, Kiel and Hanover. It is to this quarter that James returned as part of Britain's post-war occupational force, the British Army of the Rhine (BAOR). Formed from the 21st Army Group, which played a key role in the original invasion of Germany, the BAOR consisted of various military units with a total strength of 80,000 men, among them James McRory Smith.

During his period of service in the British zone, James would have played his part in helping to stabilise and rebuild Germany. Military establishments and armaments factories were dismantled and severe restrictions were placed on the development of heavy industry. Emphasis was placed upon light industry and agriculture.

In 1947 the British and American zones were merged and, by 1949, the French sector had been incorporated and the Federal Republic of Germany, or West Germany, was formed and the first federal elections took place.

During the war and in the months following VE Day fraternisation between occupying troops and the German people was prohibited. There is no doubt, however, that it did take place and relationships between British and American soldiers and German women were not uncommon. Some were short – little more than brief sexual encounters – while others endured.

James was one soldier who found love in Germany. He met a local woman and after a time they married and set up home together. Little is known about James' wife. Even his family know nothing of her, not even her name.

An obituary printed in the May 1999 edition of *Am Bratach*, a monthly news magazine published in Sutherland, following James' death notes: 'He went back into the army which took him to Germany. Here it was he met the one woman of his life and, free to marry, they settled to share their life together'.

The couple are believed to have married in the late 1940s, after Britain lifted its ban on fraternisation. They had two children, a daughter Crystal and a son, whose name is not known.

Following the sudden and unexpected death of his mother, the doubtless bloody years of conflict he endured and the return to the rubble of post-war Germany, James appears to have finally created a settled home life for himself and his new family.

But this newfound happiness was short-lived. A tragic event would befall the young family, bringing James' new life in Germany to a sudden and destructive end and settling him on the path that would ultimately lead to Strathchailleach bothy and his life as a recluse.

Again, details of the event itself are sketchy and rely heavily on anecdotal evidence. What is known is that his wife perished in a terrible road accident. It took place in Germany during the early 1950s. It is not possible to say for certain whether or not James was in the car with his wife at the time.

The *Am Bratach* obituary states: 'Poor James' wife was caught in a car crash that turned into an inferno. He had nothing left to identify her by save the rings from her fingers.'

It was clearly a very sudden and violent death. Unable to escape from the vehicle, she perished in the flames. Some say James was in the car too and although he managed to get out, he was unable to free his wife and could do little more than watch as she burned to death.

Whether or not James was present at the scene of the accident and subsequent fire, or was required to formally identify his wife's body – or rather her rings – afterwards, it was a shocking tragedy for him and a major turning point in his life.

The *Am Bratach* article adds: 'Devastated, he left Germany making for Scotland.'

This pivotal moment was the beginning of James' life on the road, a long period of wandering from one place to the next, a lonely soul seeking to escape the memory of an incident that shattered both his life and that of his young children.

The children lost not only their mother in the car crash, but also their father. As James returned to Scotland, they were taken into the care of their maternal grandparents and remained in Germany.

Like the rest of the family, James' niece Ella Connolly knows little about the accident itself. But she is convinced it set her uncle on the path that led him to become a virtual recluse.

'He must have been devastated. He lost his wife and also his children. They went to stay with their grandparents, something that would probably have happened in any family in those days. The accident must have pushed him over the edge and he just dropped out of society,' she said.

It is possible that, as a result of the accident and the violent death of his wife, James was suffering from what would today be diagnosed as Post Traumatic Stress Disorder. No one knows whether or not he sought medical advice or treatment after the accident. Even if he had, it is unlikely such a diagnosis would have been made and counselling offered.

Although descriptions of post-traumatic stress were recorded as early as the American Civil War and in 19th century train crash survivors, the term Post-Traumatic Stress Disorder was not coined until the 1980s.

Between the first and second world wars, medics identified a condition referred to as 'shell shock' or 'battle fatigue'. At this time, they believed fragments of shrapnel entering the brain caused haemorrhages that resulted in the condition. For sufferers who had not been exposed to explosions or gunfire, it was more commonly seen as a sign of weakness or a character flaw. It was not until the 1970s, and the Vietnam War, that significant research was carried out.

Post Traumatic Stress Disorder (PTSD) is a debilitating psychological condition trigged by a traumatic event. High on the list of traumatic events – and possible triggers – is serious road accidents.

According to the Royal College of Psychiatrists, a traumatic event is 'one where we can see that we are in danger, our life is threatened, or where we see other people dying or being injured. Even hearing about an unexpected injury or violent death of a family member or close friend can start PTSD'.

James responded to the tragedy by leaving Germany soon after the incident. He put physical distance between himself and the events that had led to the death of his wife. He left behind his children and the life he knew.

When he returned to Scotland, he did not seek out his family in Dumbarton. He made no contact with them. He did not return home to talk through what had happened, perhaps attempt to make some sense of the tragedy. Instead he retreated into himself, setting out on a lonely road that saw him wander the highways and byways of Scotland. He had embarked upon his life as a recluse, spending his days and nights alone, bereft of human company. To the world, he looked like a tramp. Few knew the emotional baggage he carried.

He is by no means the first or only person to retreat in this way. Following the First World War many of Britain's hermits were trench survivors suffering from shell shock. In America, after the Second World War and then the Vietnam War, some ex-servicemen, scarred by their experiences of conflict, retreated to a life of solitude in lonely, isolated places.

James returned to Scotland because it was the land he knew. With little money in his pocket, his wanderings took him first to the Perthshire town of Crieff where he found work on a farm.

At this time, James' family in Dumbarton knew nothing of the tragedy that had befallen him. Other than a brief visit after the Second World War, there had been no contact. However, in 1955, James crossed paths with his nephew Andrew Kilpatrick, albeit briefly.

Andrew was 10-years-old at the time and they met quite by chance on a country road in Argyll. The year was 1955 and Andrew was riding in the cab of his father's lorry.

'I had a day off school and I was with my old man in his lorry. We were taking a load of tar up to Oban. We had just come over the Rest and Be Thankful, near Arrochar, when we saw a guy in a long coat walking along the side of the road. He looked like a tramp but my dad seemed to recognise him. He stopped the lorry and told me it was my Uncle James,' Andrew explained.

'We picked Uncle James up and I remember sitting in the cab between him and my old man as we headed for Oban. Not much was said and we dropped him off at Connel Bridge. That was the last time anyone in the family saw or heard from Uncle James until much later.'

From Connel Bridge, James headed north to Glen Coe, securing work with the Forestry Commission, planting and felling trees. This work took him to Rannoch Forest, a large plantation east of Rannoch Moor and south west of Loch Rannoch. He found accommodation at Gorton bothy, an empty cottage six miles north of Loch Tulla and the nearest road. He stayed there for some time and it is a place he returned to many years later.

Andrew said: 'I think the Forestry Commission suited him because he was not really a people person. He liked his own space and he was able to work on his own most of the time.'

From Glen Coe, James continued his journey north, walking for much of the time, hitching a ride whenever he could. He moved from one short-term labouring job to another, rarely staying in one place for very long. He would sleep under the stars, or find shelter in abandoned cottages or derelict outbuildings. He frequently stayed in bothies used by hillwalkers but often found himself an unwelcome guest at these remote refuges, maintained as overnight shelters rather than permanent homes.

One bothy he spent some time in was Benalder Cottage, on the shores of Loch Ericht. There he met backpacker Bert Wallace, originally from Glasgow but now staying in Aberdeen.

'I was on something of a stravaig when I stopped off for a couple of nights at Benalder,' he said. 'It was the summer of 1961. I'd set off from Fort William a few days earlier, headed up to Loch Ossian and was planning an ascent of Ben Alder. The old cottage seemed like a good place to lay my head.

'When I arrived there was a guy in residence. He was a rugged, burly lad with a full beard. By the look of him, he'd been out in the wilds for quite some time.

'It was still fairly early in the day so I left my gear in the bothy and set off Ben Alder, taking in Beinn Bheoil while I was at it. It was pretty late on when I got back to the cottage and Sandy was still there.

'I made some supper and afterwards we got talking again. He regaled me with tales of derring do. I was just a young lad at the time and it all sounded pretty impressive. He told me he'd been on the road a long time, moving between bothies and abandoned cottages. I had no idea how he found them. I think he just walked until he came across somewhere he could stay. If he liked a place, he'd stay a bit longer. If he didn't, he moved on.

'He said he could walk thirty to forty miles a day, which was more than I could hope to cover on my wee trip. I remember him telling me that he could live off the land, stalking and killing deer with a knife.

'He told me he learned all that stuff in the army. He said he'd been in Germany during the war and had been in jail for two years for desertion.

'I wasn't sure how much of what he was telling me was true but he was a captivating character and all in all it was an interesting evening.

'By the time I woke the next morning he was gone. His gear was still in the cottage so I guess he had decided to spend a bit of time at Benalder. For my part, I headed on my way towards Dalwhinnie,' Bert added.

James moved from one bothy to another, often not by choice, but always heading north, as if he was intent on putting physical distance between himself and his life in Germany.

In the winter of 1962, after many long years on the road, he found himself in the wilds lands of Sutherland. The north coast was close at hand. Soon the land beneath his itinerant feet would end and he would be able to walk no further.

His journey was just about at an end. For it was here in Sutherland, in the northwest corner of Scotland, that he would settle, at a remote shepherd's cottage known as Strathchailleach.

*****

3

Strathchailleach was the sanctuary James McRory Smith so long sought. After months on the road, drifting from one labouring job to another, he finally ended his wanderings in Sutherland. The rundown cottage at Strathchailleach was not, however, to be his first home in this often wild and often inhospitable neighbourhood.

Rugged and remote, Sutherland has long held an almost hypnotic draw for those seeking solitude. The county is vast but, conversely, its population is small. It is one of the few places left in Britain where it is possible to roam all days across the hills and moors without meeting, or indeed seeing, another soul. It is as close to true wilderness as it is possible to find in the British Isles.

Much of the land was emptied of its indigenous people during the infamous Highland Clearances. Whole communities were lost as families were evicted from their rented homes - often forcibly - to make way for sheep. The Sutherland clearances started in 1812, driven by the Countess of Sutherland and her husband, the 2nd Marquis of Stafford.

Planned villages were established on the coast to house displaced inland dwellers and over the years that followed, thousands of people were decanted. Some settled in these new villages, while others left Scotland for the promise of new lives and new lands abroad.

In the winter of 1962, drawn towards Cape Wrath by this promise of isolation, James headed north, walking and hitching along the single-track road towards Durness.

He crossed the Kyle of Durness, most likely at its southern end where the water tapers into two rivers, both spanned by simple bridges, and trekked along the rough shoreline to meet the single-track road built to serve the lighthouse at Cape Wrath.

The ground here, west of the Kyle, is known as the Parph, 207 square kilometres of empty heather moor with just a smattering of small crofts. The best-known local landmark is undoubtedly the lighthouse. It was still manned by a crew of six when James arrived and the keepers, together with a handful of farming families, were the only permanent residents on the cape side of the channel.

Census records show that in 1930, 35 people lived here. But it was a dwindling population and after the Second World War, when the men left for battle and did not all return, numbers dropped to such an extent that the school was forced to close its doors for the last time in 1947.

Following its closure, the school building lay empty and abandoned, until James happened upon it. Built for education and redundant for so long, the house was far from homely. But it boasted walls and a roof and that, it seems, was all he craved. Home comforts mattered little to a man who spent so much time sleeping under the stars.

It is not known exactly how long James spent at the old Parph schoolhouse. But during his time there he earned money doing odd jobs for the Keoldale Estate, on whose land the building sat. Despite this, however, there appears to have been some local resistance to his occupation of the building. For his part, James was keen to remain in the area.

Sallie Tyszko was a close friend of James during many of the years he lived at Strathchailleach. He frequently called at her home in Kinlochbervie and, on occasion, she visited the bothy.

'He was living for a while in the old schoolhouse on the Parph but from what he told me they didn't really want him there,' she recalled. 'I think someone pointed out the bothy at Strathchailleach to him. Most of the Keoldale Estate's activities were to the north of the hills and the bothy, being to the south, was on the periphery of the estate, well away from most of the sheep. Any sheep you may see near the bothy tend to have come from the Kinlochbervie side.'

James upped sticks and hiked over the hills to Strathchailleach. In those days, he was a fit, 37-year-old man and the tramp across the barren hills and rough moor would have presented little challenge.

As the crow flies, Strathchailleach is only seven miles west of the schoolhouse where James was squatting. But it was a world away. Whereas the schoolhouse sat adjacent to a surfaced road regularly used to service the lighthouse at Cape Wrath, Strathchailleach was completely cut off, lying many miles from the nearest highway or byway. While the schoolhouse was close to other properties, Strathchailleach had no immediate neighbours. There was no one to object to him moving in.

This has always been a sparsely populated area, a wild land that has never been properly colonised. Indeed, the first maps of the area, published in the 17th century, described it as an 'extreem wilderness' infested with wolves. While people, many of them driven here like sheep during the clearances, were able to establish crofts to the northwest of Kinlochbervie, they stuck close to the coastal margins where they could access the sea for fishing, or source seaweed as fertiliser for their fields. Few ventured inland.

North of Sheigra, where the established crofts end, the shoreline consists almost entirely of cliffs. With a brief sandy interlude at Sandwood Bay, they stretch north to the lighthouse at Cape Wrath. It was this untamed and seemingly unending landscape that captured James' imagination.

Strathchailleach was by far the most remote farmstead linked to the old district of Oldshore.

Strathchailleach – James Carron

Prior to its establishment as a shepherd's cottage during the mid-19th century, the surrounding land offered good grazing for cattle.

One of the earliest written histories of the area was penned by Alexander Macrae and published by The Highland Christian Literature Society in Tongue. In his book, *Kinlochbervie*, Macrae stated that there were good grounds for believing that the district was at one time well populated and cultivated, with Strath Shinary, to the south of the bothy, offering 'good pasture for the whole district'. Early sheilings were constructed out on the moor, where the cattle were reared during the summer months, producing milk, butter and cheese. Come winter, they moved closer to the coastal crofts.

Local place names also offer strong clues to the lie of the land in pre-historic times. Much of the ground was wooded, doubtless offering cover for the wolves said to roam here. The name Strath Chailleach stems from Strath-na-Coille, the 'wooded valley', while Loch Claise na Coille (marked on the current Ordnance Survey map as Loch Claise na Coinneal), to the south of Sandwood Bay, means 'loch of the wooded valley'. Loch a' Mhuilinn translates as the 'mill loch', indicating the presence of a mill on this small stretch of water lying by the track between Blairmore and Sandwood Bay. The existence of a mill suggests a significant population lived on the land between Sheigra and Strath Shinary.

In July 1998, members of the Association of Certified Field Archaeologists from Glasgow University undertook field surveys on the Sandwood Estate, building on investigations already undertaken by the John Muir Trust, the conservation charity that owns the estate. The study concentrated on four sites, including Strath Shinary and the coastal area around Sandwood Bay.

Numerous features of archaeological interest were found at Sandwood indicating early arable cultivation that extended into the 19th and early 20th centuries. Built in the latter half of the 19th century, Sandwood House replaced an earlier longhouse-style farmstead located to the northwest and the report confirmed evidence of enclosures and an extensive early field system. However, Sandwood House and its predecessor were by no means the only structures built above the beach. At the north end of the bay, on a shelf close to the outflow of Sandwood Loch, there are the remains of an early homestead that may have been constructed by seafarers who landed here. A semi-circular enclosure initially housed a small dun-like structure and evidence on the ground indicates a larger structure later replaced this.

Ruined Sandwood House overlooking Sandwood Loch – James Carron

Inland of Sandwood Loch in Strath Shinary the remains of two distinct groups of shieling huts were found. The lower set of huts and one later house clustered around the Allt Dubh Mor, to the south of Strathan bothy. The upper group of eight structures was located just over a mile further up the glen.

Further south, at Loch Carn Mharasaid, another two groups of shieling huts were discovered, both at the east end of the lochan. Archaeological investigations suggested up to 15 separate structures on one site and another 11 on the other. It is considered unlikely, however, that so many were in use at any one time.

Inland of Blairmore and along the track to Sandwood Bay, extensive evidence of peat cutting was found, with tracks constructed specifically for this purpose. There were no traces of settlement here, possible due to the poor drainage.

The early lie of the land was subject to dramatic change in the 19th century. Following the 1819 and 1820 clearances that took place in Achumore, Strathmore, Strathbeg and, most famously, Strathnaver, many of those displaced people who did not emigrate or settle in new towns like Bettyhill, found themselves herded on to the coastal fringes between Rhiconich and Sheigra, doubling the local population within the space of just two of years. Arriving with only the possessions they could carry, or lug on horseback, they were forced to settle on rough, uncultivated patches of land not already occupied by the native people. The challenges they faced were immense, as Alexander Macrae recorded in his book.

'The land which they were allowed to reduce to a state of cultivation could not have been wrought by the plough. It was not only in a state of nature, but so rough and stony that pinch, pick and spade were the only instruments fit to be used on it. The appearance of these lands, at the present time, suggests a long process of laborious and unrenumerative effort that is extremely pathetic. The little heaps of grey stones with which these holdings are dotted, and the dykes surrounding them were dug from the patches of soil that became the fields in which they grew crops.'

The growing of crops was backbreaking and labour intensive work, but the sea offered some salvation. There was a ready supply of fish and shellfish and the crofters, more used to farming inland glens, adapted to survive. Many turned their hand to fishing, supplementing their meagre diet and giving birth to an industry that continues to this day in Kinlochbervie.

As the crofters developed their land from rough ground to arable patches, growing potatoes and barley, inevitably rents were levied on the newly reclaimed ground. But there was investment too. In 1829, the parish came under the control of the Duke of Sutherland. He commissioned the area's first road, from Kylesku to Durness, via Rhiconich. Prior to this, sea travel was the principle means of communication. The opening of the road led to the introduction a regular mail service and an inn was built at Rhiconich. With the aid of government funds, a church – the first in the district – was built in Kinlochbervie in 1829 and a school was constructed on the shoreline at Badcall Inchard, midway between Rhiconich and Kinlochbervie.

The influx of new people and improvements to the infrastructure created strong new communities within these coastal townships. But this period of stability did not last long. In 1846, a severe outbreak of potato blight hit the Highlands, wreaking havoc on harvests and leaving many families without food. Kinlochbervie was particularly hard hit.

The Duke of Sutherland declined assistance from a relief fund set up through public subscription, preferring instead to help his people. Money was provided for food and there was investment in schemes to create employment. These included the construction of a road from Rhiconich to Kinlochbervie and from there to Sheigra. Following completion of the road, a new school, built next to the road, opened at Badcall Inchard. The old one, constructed by the shore and accessed by boat, was converted into a store where meal, shipped in from Caithness, was held for distribution. An inn opened in Kinlochbervie.

The potato blight prompted the start of a wave of land clearances along the northern shore of Loch Inchard. In 1847, crofters were offered assistance to emigrate, something many must have viewed favourably in light of the prevailing famine. Many left the area aboard the *Sirius*, which sailed from Loch Laxford. Those who remained were promised larger land holdings, but in most cases this never transpired.

The land between Rhiconich and Achrisgill – 1520 acres in all – was cleared and given to the Rhiconich hotel-keeper while 1300 acres at Sheigra was cleared of its people and let as a single sheep run. At Sandwood, 1940 acres were cleared and the land was let to the tenant of Kinlochbervie Farm, a local merchant and farmer called Hugh Mackay. In the same year, the townships at Sheigra, Oldshoremore and Oldshorebeg were reorganised as crofts.

From a population of nearly 1965 in 1831, the number of people living in the parish fell to 1699 in 1841 and 10 years later it stood at 1000. According to census records, the decline continued. By 1951, there were just 787 people living in the parish.

With the destruction of crofts and the creation of large sheep runs, many of the more remote farms fell into ruin. In their place, simple shepherd's cottages were built. Bound by mortar and built using stone taken from older cottages, these were more solid structures than the simple buildings they replaced. By the mid 19th century, there were only three inhabited cottages in the vast swath of land around Sandwood and Strath Shinary. They were Strathan, Sandwood Lodge and Strathchailleach. All were home to shepherds employed to tend the sheep that now roamed where once families farmed.

The cottage at Strathchailleach was in all probability built sometime in the decade between 1841 and 1851. The earliest census information available for the district, collected in 1841, makes no mention of Strathchailleach. There is only reference to a cottage at Shinary, most likely Strathan, which at that point was home to a 53-year-old shepherd, his wife and their five children.

A decade later, the census taker recorded a cottage at 'Strath Chailleach'. In that year it was home to 56-year-old shepherd William Morrison, his 54-year-old wife Elisa, their sons George (26) and John (18) and daughter Bell (23). The offspring are all described as scholars.

The 1861 census recorded the cottage as 'Strath Challach House'. Mr Morrison and his wife and daughter remained in residence, joined by Mr Morrison's brother, John, a 61-year-old fisherman who was widowed, and his daughter Bell, who was 18.

In 1871, 'Strath Calloch' was home to Duncan McDonald, a 24-year-old shepherd, his wife Robina (21) and the couple's one-year-old daughter Lexy. Also in residence was Mr McDonald's sister, Houghina, who was single and described as a domestic servant, and Mrs McDonald's 13-year-old sister, Barbara McKenzie.

Ten years later 'Strath Calloch' was again occupied by a shepherd, this time 36-year-old Donald McCasgill, his wife Isabella (34) and their one-year-old daughter Williamina.

The 1891 census referred to the cottage as 'Strathcallach' and described it as an uninhabited 'shepherd's house'. This period of disuse appears only to have been temporary as, in the latter years of the 19th century, Norman Morrison's family lived there for a short period before moving to Sandwood Lodge, two miles to the south.

'My mother was born in 1897 at Strathchailleach, and then moved with the rest of her family to Sandwood Lodge, leaving there for Lewis at the age of eight,' Norman recalled.

'Both she and several of my aunts and uncles lived at Sandwood Bay and spoke with great affection and awe of the place but, as so often happens, we, the next generation, did not listen to all that was being said and consequently did not ask enough questions.

'What does stick in my memory is my mother's description of feeding the hens with salmon and the beautiful and spacious beach. Sandwood Bay, when I saw it after that trudge from Blairmore, lived up to all expectations. It amazed me how people managed to transport their belongings and provisions to such an isolated location. Even the registration of my mother's birth at Kinlochbervie involved my grandfather in a whole day's journey.

'By today's standards, living in such isolation would be regarded as something of a trial. Not so for my mother and her siblings. They had such happy memories of the place, most of which, unfortunately, they took with them.'

Sandwood Bay – James Carron

Strathchailleach's location may have been remote and the surrounding land rough, but a slither of flat land adjacent to the Strath Chailleach river was fertile enough to grow crops and keep livestock on and, despite the disappearance of every last branch of timber in what was once a heavily wooded valley, the moor did offer a steady supply of peat for burning.

The earliest Ordnance Survey map of the area, surveyed in 1873, shows a cottage and a separate outbuilding at 'Strath na Caillich'. Surveyed again the following year, the cottage and outbuilding are shown sitting in an enclosure of land bounded to the north by a bend in the river.

The 1878 map of the area reveals a farmstead, comprising two roofed buildings, two unroofed structures and three enclosures while the 1908 OS survey shows the addition of a bridge over the Strath Chailleach, adjacent to the cottage. The OS survey of 1927/28 names the cottage as 'Strachallach' and again shows a house, outbuilding and bridge.

The last available census information, for 1901, reveals that 'Strathcalloch House' was home to Angus Maclean, a shepherd and a single man. Thereafter there is only anecdotal evidence of occupation suggesting the last permanent residents – prior to the arrival of James McRory Smith – lived at Strathchailleach during the 1930s and early 1940s. The occupants are believed to have been a family who left when their children reached school age.

The cottage was certainly empty in the mid-1950s when Bernard Heath, a stalwart of the Mountain Bothies Association, and Frank Goodwin, of Huddersfield, cycled from Sandwood Bay to Cape Wrath. Recounting the trip in the MBA's newsletter of March 1999, Bernard described the cottage as 'unlocked, clean and tidy.' At this point, the cottage was first identified as a possible candidate for MBA stewardship. However, James McRory Smith beat the organisation to it.

Finding Strathchailleach in a good state of repair and, more importantly, empty, he moved in. In the early 1960s, the cottage stood pretty much as it does today, although there has been some maintenance and repair work carried out over the years. Occupying a shallow trough that affords some shelter, it is a squat structure, built low to the ground from rough stone and lime mortar. Back then, as today, it had an iron roof. The front elevation has two windows and a low door, so low in fact that even those of average height have to stoop to enter. Attached to the western gable there was a barn, but it has long been ruined.

The bothy sits on the Keoldale Estate, 27,061 acres of land owned by the Scottish Government's Rural Affairs Department. It is a crofting estate managed by the Keoldale Sheepstock Club, a Friendly Society set up in 1926 to represent the 40 or so tenants who live on and work the land and are effectively shareholders of the collectively operated sheep stock club.

To the south, the closest road is six miles off and it is no major highway, just a narrow single-track road serving crofts spreading west from Kinlochbervie, ending on the shores of the Atlantic. The journey into Strathchailleach is a long trek over pitted tracks and uneven paths. Prior to 1993, when the John Muir Trust bought Sandwood Estate, it was possible to drive as far as Loch a'Mhuilinn, where the track from Blairmore ends. From here, a path continues for two miles to Sandwood Bay, passing above the ruin of Sandwood Lodge, which overlooks Sandwood Loch.

To reach Strathchailleach from here, one must cross the bay and negotiate the outflow from the loch. Although relatively wide, the stream, in normal conditions, is not particularly deep and can be safely forded in Wellington boots. After heavy rain or snow, however, it presents a considerably more challenging obstacle and the nearest bridge is to be found at Strathan, three miles up Strath Shinary, beyond the head of Sandwood Loch.

From the river, a rough pony track once existed to Strathchailleach. It rose over rough heather hillside to Lochan nan Sac before descending into the valley of Strath Chailleach. Through lack of use, the moor has gradually reclaimed this trail and today it is only recognisable in places.

When the last occupants pulled shut the door on Strathchailleach in the 1940s, the cottage was not, as so many others were in these parts, abandoned to the elements and allowed to fall into ruin. It was maintained in a wind and watertight state by the estate as a simple refuge, intended primarily for shepherds. None were posted there permanently, but it did offer shelter for occasional overnight stays or lunch breaks. Hillwalkers and anglers also used it for this purpose.

So James would have found a building in a generally good state of repair, with two main rooms and a smaller bedroom to the rear of the building. The more easterly of the two larger rooms, accessed from a tiny lobby behind the front door, boasted an open fire with a simple grate. There was no electricity and no running water, no kitchen and no bathroom. All who had gone before him took their water direct from the Strath Chailleach river. By today's standards it was primitive, a hovel even, but the front door and windows were in place, and the roof kept the rain and, in winter, the snow out.

By the time James arrived, the once fertile parcel of land stretching west from the cottage was waterlogged and beset with reeds and the neighbouring barn was slowly crumbling away. But he never entertained any notion of a crofting life and, by all accounts, had no plans to return Strathchailleach to a working farm. He was more of a forager than a farmer. His primary interest was the cottage and its unchallenged solitude.

*****

4

James McRory Smith quickly made Strathchailleach his home. When he moved in, there may very well already have been some rudimentary items of furniture, seats and tables used by shepherds, hikers and fishermen who occasionally visited the old cottage. He wasted no time in adding to these and spent much of his time foraging through the flotsam on the beach at Sandwood Bay, gathering anything washed up on the tide that he could make use of.

The sea would prove to be one of his main providers and wooden fish and fruit boxes were particularly useful catches. These formed the basis for much of his furniture and, using incredibly ingenuity and a fair amount of scavenged fence wire, he also fashioned them into a bridge over the Strath Chailleach, after he tired of constantly fording the stream. His simple bridges were frequently washed out, but James tirelessly rebuilt them time and time again over the years.

The abandoned boxes were also a ready source of fuel for the fire and when times were particularly hard, it was not unknown for him to hack up some of his precious furniture to keep the cold at bay. Despite once being heavily wooded, the Strath Chailleach valley was tree-less when James arrived and there were no forests within easy reach of the bothy, only vast expanses of heather, grass and marsh. The nearest woodland is two miles to the southwest, on the opposite side of Sandwood Loch. So fish boxes and other wood washed ashore were vital to James if he was to keep his home fire burning. All of it had to be carried or dragged for over a mile back to Strathchailleach.

James also cut and dried peat from the moor, stacking it up against the cottage's eastern gable in the weeks and months leading up to the autumn and winter. Just downstream of the bothy, a natural slip in the land exposed a large bank of sheltered peat from which he took his fuel, following in the footsteps of the cottage's many previous residents who relied on this nature resource.

James McRory Smith – Howard Patrick

The recluse soon settled in to his bothy. The eastern room of the cottage, the one with the fireplace, became his sitting room. It is a small, poky, almost claustrophobic chamber with a low ceiling and a tiny, deep-set, window that peers myopically out on to the hillside. The external walls and ceiling were plastered while the interior partitions were wooden. At night, he bedded down on a hard mattress of fishboxes and old woollen blankets, in the tiny backroom. Another small window peeking out across the river told him whether it was light or dark outside.

The other main room he left empty for the shepherds who occasionally called. At that time, it was in a simple state with only a hard earth floor and rough, unrefined walls. It was of no use to James. He was content to confine himself to two rooms and doubtless could have survived in one, if it were the only option open to him.

With no electricity or running water, James relied on the fire for heat and candles for light. He took his water straight from the Strath Chailleach, which runs adjacent to the bothy, and the vast expanse of moor surrounding the building was effectively his toilet. He washed in a bucket or, if the weather was warm, the stream, which doubled as his laundry.

In addition to cutting peat and foraging for wood, James was kept busy stocking his larder. A large part of his diet consisted of fish, caught using a rod and line. The land around Strathchailleach is dotted with lochans and smaller pools that have long attracted anglers. The closest to the bothy are Lochan nan Sac and Loch a'Gheodha Ruaidh, but James also ventured further up the Strath Chailleach, to Loch a'Phuill Bhuidhe, below Creag Riabhach, one of the highest peaks in the area. Trout was his main catch.

One entry in the MBA's bothy logbook for Strathchailleach recalled a visit made by one hillwalker who spotted the hermit hard at work during the winter. It read: 'I met James striding through the snow with his shirt unbuttoned, oblivious to the cold. I watched him walk up the glen from a pool downstream of the bothy carrying a fly rod. I arrived back at the bothy at 3.30am to find him sitting outside by a small heather fire, two trout in the pan.'

All cooking was done over an open fire, using wood, peat and clumps of heather, and any rubbish generated was either burned or dumped within the confines of the ruined outbuilding. There were no council rubbish collections at Strathchailleach.

James supplemented his diet with shellfish gathered at Sandwood Bay. He also hunted and trapped hare and occasionally small deer on the moor. On one occasion he was fortunate to find a recently deceased stag snared in the remains of an old fence upstream from the bothy. There was also a plentiful supply of rabbits on the craggy slopes bordering the north shore of nearby Sandwood Loch and sometimes visiting shepherds or hillwalkers would donate leftover food.

It was a simple life and James enjoyed few luxuries, other than cigarettes – he was a heavy smoker and his favourite brand was Capstan Full Strength – and a wee dram or a can of beer. High Commissioner whisky and Carlsberg Special Brew were his drinks of choice.

Hillwalker Rod Shepherd was a regular visitor to the bothy and he enjoyed several conversations with James, all of them at the fireside with a glass of whisky in hand.

'James was a very frugal man and didn't seem interested in personal possessions. As long as he had his radio, something to read and his cigarettes and whisky he was content,' Rod explained.

'At night, batteries permitting, he liked to listen to the radio. He listened to football commentaries, political debates and the like. Despite living so far out of society, he always kept in touch with what was happening. He was very interested in what was happening beyond his front door.

'He also had books and magazines. I'm not sure where he got them from but he was an avid reader. I suppose it helped him fill the long nights, particularly during the winter when he didn't get out as much. It probably helped him stay sane. When he had finished reading the magazines, he would cut out pictures he liked and he glued them to the walls as a form of decoration or used them as the basis for his own paintings.

'Although he was not always particularly welcoming to visitors and had a wee bit of a reputation on that front, there were times when he enjoyed a little bit of company, a chat over a drink. Indeed, there were occasions when he would walk north to the lighthouse at Cape Wrath and spend a few hours with the keepers, just chatting over a cup of tea.

'Even though he could be quite convivial, especially after a few drinks, he rarely opened up about himself or revealed much about his past. He was happy enough to talk about the present and his life at the bothy but when I asked why he had decided to live at Strathchailleach, he just said he wanted to escape the rat race. He didn't elaborate.

'He loved the great outdoors, particularly the fact he could wander at will for hours, sometimes days, at a time, and he took a keen interest in nature. He kept himself busy and always seemed to be on the go, either fishing or scouring the beach at Sandwood.

'He was the first to admit that it was a hard life, particularly in the winter. But he never expressed any regrets and said he always planned to see his days out at Strathchailleach.

The main room in Strathchailleach bothy – James Carron

'He said he enjoyed the simple life and in a way I envied that. Although there were pressures on him, most of them environmental, he didn't have to worry about work, or paying the rent or bills.'

Life at Strathchailleach was indeed free of rent, rates or utility bills. James never owned or leased the cottage and was effectively a squatter. But other than as an occasional refuge for shepherds, its owners, the Keoldale Estate, had no use for the building and did not oppose his occupation. In return, James looked after the bothy, tending to minor repairs and maintaining it, as best he could, in a wind and watertight state.

Another visitor to the bothy was former Royal Marine John Slater who sought respite from the rain at Strathchailleach during a mammoth round Britain trek in 1976. He was welcomed in by the hermit and gave a fascinating account of James' home life at the time.

'During a most memorable walk from the Cape Wrath lighthouse to Kinlochbervie – visibility was negligible due to horrendous rain and mist – I had to cross several severely rain-swollen rivers, one of them was in Strath Chailleach,' he recalled. 'Out of the mist, as I walked with my Labrador, appeared a very small and seemingly half demolished bothy cottage with a small fast flowing stream close to the front door.

'Anyone in?' I shouted above the storm.

'Come in,' roared a voice from within.

'This is not what I had expected but any chance of shelter and maybe a blether with another human being who obviously shared my love of remote places had the potential for another interesting entry in my day to day diary jottings.

'I entered the low front door after crossing the small wooden bridge made entirely of old fish boxes – wooden in those days – and fencing wire. It was seriously dark within, the only light coming from a fireplace that was seriously clogged with wood ash and in which languished a smouldering, not too welcoming section of damp tree root.

'The small room was quite smoke filled and it took me a moment or two to focus on the soul occupant. This was Sandy. He was quite small and wiry. The voice when he first spoke suggested a condition of the throat brought about by a long term addiction to tobacco and his demeanour also suggested a dram or two may very well have kept his company prior to my unexpected arrival.

'I was able to establish after shaking his hand firmly in greeting that he had read all about my coastal walk for charity and he knew I was in the area.

'There was no phone, no toilet and apparently no water facility. Chaos reined. The only chair was a battered relative of the wooden bridge outside over which I had arrived. Books and old magazines were stacked in random piles against the walls, an old raincoat hung dripping on the back of the front door and only a small wooden table on which stood a couple of mugs made up this spartan scene.

'My vision immediately focussed on the astonishing artwork in the ceiling. Painted in garish gloss paints and partly hidden by years of nicotine pollution, I could make out planets, stars and strange squiggled letters that conveyed absolutely nothing to me.

'Sandy asked me about my walk and offered me a dram and we talked for some time over a cup of tea. I was astounded to learn that he lived permanently in this strange tumbledown little bothy, trapped in an environment that filled every waking moment of every day with nature at her most beautiful.

'I said goodbye to Sandy after we had finished a good hot cup of tea and he gave me a cheese sandwich to take with me. I sneaked a five-pound note under my empty cup on the table which I sensed would be better delivered that way by way of thanks, and stepped outside. The rain had stopped, there appeared a break in the clouds and misty sunlight struggled to caress my face.

'I never returned but I did leave wondering just who Sandy was, apart from a genuinely reclusive individual.'

A reclusive individual he may have been, but to survive at Strathchailleach, James was unable to cut himself off completely from society. He had to make regular trips, on foot, to Kinlochbervie to buy essential provisions, such as candles, batteries for his small radio, food and drink. To fund this, he relied on unemployment benefit payments and, in later years, the state pension, collected in person from the Post Office at Balchrick.

This weekly round trek of 26-miles was James' only regular contact with the outside work, other than his radio. Come rain, hail or shine, he set off at first light, following the rough former pony track linking the bothy with Sandwood Bay. After fording the outflow of Sandwood Loch, an at times treacherous task, he trekked across the beach, climbed through the dunes to the ruin of Sandwood Lodge and continued over the track to join the public road at Blairmore. A short walk west took him to Balchrick Post Office, where he collected his money.

Bridget Graham is the postmistress at Balchrich where the Post Office is housed in a small wooden shed attached to her house.

'He came in once a fortnight to attend to his business,' she said. 'My father, who was postmaster before me, used to look after him, as many people in the area did. Even when he moved into a caravan in Kinlochbervie he continued to come here for his money.

James McRory Smith at Balchrich Post Office – Howard Patrick

'Once he had attended to his business, he would walk or hitch a lift down to Kinlochbervie. Often people on the road would have little choice about offering him a lift. He would stand in the road in front of them, forcing them to stop and pick him up,' she added.

Arriving in Kinlochbervie, James frequently called on Sallie Tyszko, who moved to the area in 1977 and became a close friend.

'He was a lovely man and he always came out of the hills really clean, with clean hair and a clean shirt on. He was never scruffy or dirty,' she explained.

'He always stopped off at my house – it was the first one on the way into Kinlochbervie – for a cup of tea or a bowl of soup. When he came in it was like he had all of that big open skyness in his being. He had the whole of that wide-open place in his heart.

'For someone who lived such a solitary life, he wasn't at all nervous or reluctant about coming out. In fact whenever he came down he

47

always talked a lot. He had a lot to say and it was as if he had bottled it all up in his head and when he came into town it all just poured out.'

From Kinlochbervie, James continued along the road to Badcall where he shopped for provisions at London Stores, a tiny and rather old fashioned general grocery shop stocked floor to ceiling with food, drink and household goods. His shopping list – which he wrote on scraps of paper or old envelopes – tended to consist of 'porridge, potatoes and greens'. With the rest of his money he bought cigarettes, beer and whisky.

On his return home, he usually called at the Kinlochbervie Hotel (formerly the Garbet Hotel) for a drink. Here he would also try and secure a lift back to Blairmore and, if possible, along the track as far as Loch a'Mhuilinn.

The supply run brought James into contact with local people and local opinion of him appears to have been divided between those who had little time for the hermit and those who respected his unusual lifestyle and went out of their way to help him in any way they could.

Sallie continued: 'There were certainly some people in the area who looked out for him. People looked after him. They appreciated the long distances he walked and knew what the hills in which he lived were like. There was a degree of respect, although he was a bit of a rogue at times.'

Many people, however, had more to worry about than the appearance of a stranger in their midst. In the early 1960s, when James arrived in Kinlochbervie, he found himself living on the edge of a community at the crossroads. Economically, the area was depressed, suffering, as many other parts of the Highland were, from worrying levels of migration, particularly amongst the younger members of its population.

By today's standards, living in a desolate cottage without running water or electricity is highly unusual, if not unique. But in the late 1960s and early 1970s it was not beyond the comprehension of the local population, particularly those occupying the scattered crofts of Oldshore. Although served by mains electricity and water, power

48

cuts were frequent and the water supply was inadequate, regularly drying up when demand was high. Indeed some cottages, including the one occupied by Sallie Tyszko, were not even connected to the national grid.

For decades the parish of Eddrachillis, in which Kinlochbervie sits, had relied on crofting for employment. But the returns were increasingly poor, forcing many people to leave the area in search of work. As a result, it was an increasingly ageing sector of the community that derived its income from the land and many needed second jobs just to stay afloat. More worryingly for the future of the local population, in Oldshoremore and Sheigra, no women below the age of 45 remained.

New forestry projects were creating some of these much-sought jobs and, in the 1950s significant strides were made in securing a viable future for Kinlochbervie's fishing industry. MacBraynes constructed the first pier on Loch Clash at the end of the 19th century for their steamers and in 1928 a new concrete pier was installed. Following the Second World War, concerted efforts were made by the Garbet Estate and the County Council to encourage herring landings, creating onshore work for local women who salted and packed the catches. A co-ordinated system of lorry transport was also put in place to whisk the fish off to market.

In the 1950s white fish took over from herring as the main catch landed at Loch Clash and a new ice-making plant was installed at the harbour. In 1963 this was replaced by a modern electrically operated ice-making plant and the value of white fish – mainly haddock, cod and whiting – landed at Kinlochbervie steadily increased. However, all but one of the boats using the harbour was based on the east coast, so while fishing was seen as a major growth industry, it had yet to deliver significant local employment with those jobs already created confined to quayside activities.

More dynamic action was needed, as an economic study of the area undertaken in 1964 confirmed. The *Report of the Survey of the Parishes of Assynt and Eddrachillis*, by AW Adam and I Rankin concluded: 'The parishes of Assynt and Eddrachillis are remote in position, limited in resources, and under-developed by national standards. They are in urgent need of a planned programme of regional rehabilitation, and if viable communities are to survive in them, considerably more vigorous measures of development than are at present in force are essential.

'Severely limited opportunities have led to the continued emigration of men of ability and enterprise and the estates which hold all the land have been mainly interested in sporting rights… in these circumstances development initiated within the area in modern times has been very inadequate.

'Crofting agriculture is in dire need of reorganisation and improvement, and on the estates encouragement should be given to the landowners to make fullest use by means of stock farms and forestry. The fishing industry should be maintained and fostered, and the expansion of local interests encouraged.'

The report also highlighted the importance of tourism to the area's future.

'Tourism is now of great significance in the economy, but because of its seasonal character it cannot in itself be a foundation for prosperity. Various improvements in facilities are required, and the benefits from a better-developed tourist industry would permeate all sections of the economy,' the report added.

In the 1960s, the majority of guests at the Garbet Hotel were anglers, but, according to the authors, there existed the potential to attract hillwalkers, climbers and those engaged in nature studies. On a more positive note, they found that a number of crofters were taking advantage of government grants to establish bed and breakfast businesses, or create holiday chalets on their land.

As a keen hillwalker, Alistair Currie would have fitted perfectly into the tourism target group highlighted by the report. He visited in 1968 with a group of climbing friends and was immediately intrigued by mention of a local hermit. James McRory Smith was clearly a subject of local conversation and, as Alistair explained, there was a healthy dose of speculation as to why he had chosen to settle in such a remote spot.

'We stayed in the bothy at Sandwood Lodge,' he said. 'In those days it still had half a roof so shelter could be found. We heard from locals that some years previously an unfriendly hermit had taken up residence in the bothy at Strathchailleach.

'The story was told that the hermit had moved from the shipyards of Glasgow during the Cuban missile crisis, believing there would be a nuclear war and the safest place to be was on the north west coast of the British mainland where the prevailing winds off the Atlantic Ocean would blow the fallout back across Europe.'

Whether this was a story James himself had told, or was a product of local gossip is not known. The reference to an unfriendly hermit does, however, highlight some local attitudes to James at the time. But it did not deter Alistair Currie from seeking him out.

'We stayed for about a week and one afternoon, as the weather was not good for much else, I went for a walk on my own and deliberately ended up at the hermit's cottage,' he continued.

'I must admit I was feeling apprehensive as I knocked at the door. But it was opened and I was given a real Highland welcome. He showed me to his couch, which was cleverly made out of fish boxes, as was all the furniture he had. The seating had what appeared to be travelling rugs on them. It was cold and miserable outside while inside a good fire warmed the room.

'It took only minutes for him to offer tea and cake which he had made. After this there appeared strong home brew. I delved into my pack and produced the remains of the previous night's malt whisky.

'We sat and talked and drank for four of five hours. He told me he had stocked a small lochan over the burn with rainbow trout, but he wouldn't tell me which one.

'At this time in his life I found him to be very welcoming, talkative and good company.'

During his early years at Strathchailleach, James created as comfortable an existence for himself as he could and, despite his reputation as the 'unfriendly hermit' among some sections of the community, he could be a genial host on his home turf, as visits by Alistair Currie, John Slater and Rod Shepherd illustrate.

He also appears to have been undaunted by the change of the seasons, adapting quickly to the demands of winter when temperatures often plunged below zero and the bothy was frequently engulfed by deep, drifting snow and battered by fierce blizzards.

In summer, he was happiest out of doors and often spent many days away from Strathchailleach, trekking the moors, sleeping rough under the stars and sometimes staying overnight at another open bothy, Strathan, a few miles to the west. Occasional forays were even made as far east as Dornoch and Dingwall, James travelling on foot or hitching a ride where he could.

On fair days he wore trousers and a shirt while inclement weather brought out a long, oilskin coat. Whatever the weather, he always sported Wellington boots and either a flat cap or woollen bonnet.

In winter James was frequently confined to the cottage for many days at a time, imprisoned by the elements. To collect water from the Strath Chailleach, he sometimes had to hack through thick ice to fill his bucket. He occupied his waking hours reading books, magazines and newspapers, painting, or listening to his radio.

It is a mark of the strength of his character that he was able to endure such extreme and inhospitable physical conditions, particularly those wreaked upon him during the long, cold winter months when he lived without central heating, hot water or even, when times were really bad, a good meal. James was definitely a survivor and a notable exception. Others have tried and failed to make a go of it in similar circumstances in the same barren part of Scotland.

In September 1990, a couple unofficially took up residence at Strathan bothy, an equally basic cottage again without running water, electricity or a road connection with the outside world. After carting in their furniture and a menagerie of animals, Robbie Northway and his wife Ann set out to return the cottage to a working croft. But while the Keoldale Estate raised no opposition to James McRory Smith's occupation of Strathchailleach, it was different story for the Northway's at Strathan.

Crofters, who derived much of their income from sheep, expressed concern over the presence of the couple's dogs and the Mountain Bothies Association voiced opposition to their unofficial occupation of its bothy. A removal notice was issued on behalf of the landowner, the Scottish Executive, but the couple appealed against this. The case came to court on January 8 of the following year and at Dornoch, Sheriff Ian Cameron found they had no case to oppose the order, as they had no title to the property.

A notice to quit was delivered by sheriff officers who, accompanied by police and a representative of the MBA, tramped four miles on foot over the rough path from Oldshore to the bothy. Mr Northway left amicably, his wife having already departed, and the building was secured.

Like Strathchailleach, Strathan has long been a shepherd's cottage and like Strathchailleach it is a simple structure built from rough stone and roofed with corrugated iron. The 1841 census referred to the cottage as Shinary but come the next population survey in 1851 it was named as Strathan, home to a 56-year-old shepherd, his three sons and one daughter.

Strathan bothy – James Carron

Unlike Strathchailleach, however, Strathan appears to have had a more stable occupancy, as shepherd John Morrison and his wife Margaret were resident there for at least 20 years, appearing on census records for 1861, 1871 and 1881. In 1861 and 1871, they were living with Mr Morrison's ageing aunt, Henny, described as single and a pauper, and Jean McKay, a 19-year-old domestic servant. By 1881, however, the aunt was gone and the couple, aged 47 and 46 respectively, had two children, a son George (17) and a daughter Elizabeth (11). They continued to employ a domestic servant, 19-year-old Angesica McKenzie.

The 1891 census recorded shepherd John McKay (40), his wife Johan (38) and their five children, aged between one and 11, as tenants. At the time of the census, assistant shepherd Hugh Campbell was also staying at Strathan. Mr McKay and his children William, Joseph, John, Georgina and Barbara, appeared again on the 1901 census.

Like Strathchailleach, Strathan passed into the care of the Mountain Bothies Association and continues to be used as a refuge by hillwalkers and anglers. James McRory Smith was a regular visitor, sometimes staying overnight. Of particularly use to him was the bridge below the bothy, the only reliable point at which he could cross the river flowing west through Strath Shinary. It runs through Sandwood Loch to join the Atlantic Ocean at Sandwood Bay. When water levels were low, James was able to ford the water at the bay. However, during heavy rain it often became impassable and he was forced to hike to Strathan to make the crossing safely.

Another more tragic case highlights just how difficult it is to survive in this remote part of Sutherland. In December 2002, a 39-year-old woman was found starving at another bothy, just a few miles north of Strathchailleach. Like James McRory Smith, Margaret Davies, a writer and artist, had set out in search of isolation. She walked north from Fort William, following the Cape Wrath Trail. Her self-contained hike ended at Kervaig, a small cottage located about three miles east of the cape.

It offered the perfect spot for the Cambridge-educated geographer's treatise on the nature of solitude. But for Davies, an experienced independent traveller, it was home for just a few weeks. With little in the way of rations, she soon ran out of food. Despite this, she remained in residence, growing weaker by the day as starvation set in.

Two local shepherds who were bringing in their remaining sheep for the winter found her lying almost unconscious within the bitterly cold cottage. Hamish Campbell and his colleague Alistair Sutherland had stopped off at the bothy for a bite of lunch.

'It was lovely weather and we discussed whether to have our sandwiches outside,' Hamish Campbell recalled. 'But the bothy door was ajar, which is unusual because normally the people who use it are careful to keep it secure. We went in and there she was, lying on the makeshift bed. I didn't know if she was alive or dead, but then I saw her throat moving and I put my hand on her. She was terribly anaemic and emaciated. She moaned and raised her arm.'

Kervaig bothy – Gilbert Campbell

Sutherland set off towards the lighthouse to raise the alarm while Campbell lit a fire with some old newspapers and attempted to comfort the semi-conscious woman.

'She couldn't speak. I told her that Alistair had gone for help but I think she was beyond understanding.'

Help soon arrived and Davies was airlifted by coastguard helicopter to the Western Isles Hospital in Stornoway. She died two days later. The cause of her death was given as hypothermia.

'I've no idea what happened to her,' says Hamish Campbell. 'She had left that note on the windowsill and there were others by the bed. But usually people bring more supplies than they need. She said she was thirsty but there was water right by her.'

A search of the bothy revealed no food, just discarded biscuit wrappers, used tea bags and two empty packs of dried rations. Her parents believe that their daughter's death was the consequence of a tragic misjudgement.

'She liked to experience hardship,' said her mother Wendy, 'And it wasn't out of character for her to stretch herself far. She often came back from travelling very thin.'

It remains a mystery why Davies did not walk out to Durness while she still had the strength to do so. The 15-minute hike up what is a fairly steep and rough track to the road at the top may have deterred her. One theory is that in a weakened state and with no guarantee of help at the top of the track, she decided to conserve what little energy she had left and remain in the relative shelter of the bothy, perhaps hoping someone would call. A scribbled note found on one of the windowsills read: 'Running low on food and dry milk. Willing to pay anyone who can bring food.'

She may, of course, have surrendered to the advanced stages of hypothermia, the symptoms of which can include lethargy, confusion and, most dangerous of all, a euphoric denial on the part of the sufferer that there is anything wrong.

During her trek, Davies would undoubtedly have passed by Strathchailleach on the final leg of the trail from Sandwood Bay to Cape Wrath. There is no record, however, as to whether she stopped off at the bothy.

These, of course, are isolated and exceptional incidents. But the case of Margaret Davies in particular does highlight just how difficult it is to survive in such an unforgiving place, particularly in the depths of winter. She had travelled widely, staying in such hostile environments as Afghanistan and Nepal. Yet it was the wilds of Sutherland that ultimately defeated her.

Strathchailleach is not unlike Kervaig. If anything it is more isolated and more difficult to access. Yet James McRory Smith was able to survive here for over three decades.

His survival, however, was not simply a case of overcoming physical challenges. There were mental challenges too and, for James, these were often far more difficult to confront.

*****

5

Many people who encountered James in the early years, whether in Kinlochbervie or as a visitor to his bothy, saw him as a hard man, a physically strong individual who used his bodily strength to survive in the harsh environment he called home.

Outwardly at least, he did indeed present a formidable figure. A photograph of James taken in 1976, when he was 51 years of age, shows a solid, muscular man. His face, framed by jet-black hair and a neatly cropped black beard, is red and heavily lined. His inquisitive eyes peer out from beneath a furrowed brow. His strong hands are heavily engrained with the dark hue of hard physical labour.

James McRory Smith in 1976 – Sallie Tyszko

To strangers he was a man of few words who rarely smiled. He seldom, if ever, talked about his past, about his early years in Dumbarton, his war service or the tragic death of his wife. But over the years plenty of rumours bubbled up to fill this void and many supported the image of a hard man.

Stories are told not only in Kinlochbervie but further a field in the Scottish Highlands of a hard drinking, rough and tumble former steelworker who endured the rigours of the shipbuilding industry. Others say James was a Special Forces commando responsible for daring and, at times, bloodthirsty wartime deeds and there are those who believe he kept a Lee Enfield pistol at Strathchailleach. Many such stories are simply the product of local gossip and furtive imaginations with no factual evidence to support them.

There is no doubt James was a hard man. He had to be to endure the long, cold winters at Strathchailleach. It is fair to assume that he had witnessed a lot of pain and suffering in his life, both on the battlefields of northern Europe and in Germany after the war. But he needed great mental strength too to cope in such an isolated place, devoid as he was of human company for much of the time. Whether the years on the road helped dull the memory of his dead wife and, before her, his dead mother will never be known. Maybe Strathchailleach offered a clean sheet, a new start. It is unlikely, however, that James could ever have forgotten what happened in his past.

To an extent, alcohol played a part in dulling the pain of these bitter memories. He was known to be a heavy drinker, frequently embarking upon lengthy binges, some of them lasting several days. But alcohol alone could not help him cope with the mental challenges of such a reclusive lifestyle. There were long hours of day and night to fill and here his many and varied interests sustained him.

There was a gentle, creative side to his nature. We know that as a boy, James devoted much of his energy to painting and drawing, an interest he continued to pursue at Strathchailleach. In his early years, free from the interference of urban street lighting, he studied the night sky above the cottage in detail and replicated it on the ceiling within his main living room. Visitors like former Royal Marine John Slater were impressed by the level of detail James achieved despite only having household gloss paint to work with.

Over the years further images appeared on the walls of the bothy and some remain to this day, an enduring legacy of his occupation. The wooden internal walls he covered with colourful patterns. On the plaster of the external walls, he painted more detailed images, using oil paints and brushes left to him by both friends and passing strangers.

To the left of the fireplace, James rendered the wall with a painting of a lady playing the harp. It is a remarkably detailed and well-composed piece. To the right of the grate he created a series of small scenes include a red deer stag and wildcat, a Viking long ship and a girl carrying on her back a large bag. On the back wall of the living room there are further tableau depicting Neptune, a man with a bow and arrow and an Indian girl.

Painting of a lady with a harp – James Carron

The artwork continued into James' tiny back bedroom where wooden panels provided the canvas for larger pictures including one of a chestnut brown horse and another showing an Indian girl with a papoose. Again, these remain in place. James also painted pictures on pages torn from old magazines. These were pinned to internal walls but were lost over time.

Scenes like the stag and wildcat may have been inspired by sightings made within the landscape that surrounded him, but the majority of his paintings featured more exotic content he can only have seen in magazines or books.

While James' murals remain on the walls at Strathchailleach, some of his work left with visitors, traded for food, cigarettes, alcohol, books or magazines. Word of his talent was not confined to the bothy and, according to his sister Winnie, it was not unusual for people who knew of his artistic ability to hike up to Strathchailleach with paper and paint and a request that he draw for them. To a man living on little money, it was an opportunity to put his creative skills to profitable use.

'He was very good at drawing and many people who visited him went away with some of his drawings,' Winnie said. 'Some people would bring him canvas and oil paints and ask him to paint for them.'

James would retain the brushes and what paint remained, allowing him to focus on the subjects that interested him most. In addition to painting, he was an avid reader and, at times, the main room of the bothy was cluttered with magazines and books.

As John Slater recalled in 1976: 'Books and magazines were stacked in random piles against the walls.'

Another visitor to Strathchailleach in the 1970s was angler Steve Moss, from Edinburgh. He recalls a similar scene.

'I knew nothing of the bothy when I set off for a few days fishing in the far north in the summer of 1979,' he said. 'However, I had heard that the lochans between Sandwood Bay and Cape Wrath were very good for trout fishing and, in particular, brown trout.

James McRory Smith with his artwork at Strathchailleach – Howard Patrick

'I packed my tent and camping gear into the car and headed north to Kinlochbervie. I drove as far as I could up the track towards the bay and in those days it was possible to park by Loch a'Mhuilinn so I left the car there and continued on foot.

'I pitched my tent in the dunes between Sandwood Bay and Sandwood Loch. I remember it was a glorious spot, with an endless view out to sea. I had arrived late in the day so it was the next morning before I started to explore the area properly.

'Unfortunately, as is often the way in the Highlands, the weather was dismal. The cloud that morning was low and it was drizzling. But I set off nonetheless, hiking north, aiming for a couple of the larger lochans I had identified on my map.

'I made it over the river at the top end of the beach without any problem but the ground beyond was very rough and there was no sign of a path. I couldn't see much so I was relying on my compass to lead me in the right direction.

'I knew I would have to cross the river in Strath Chailleach and I can't recall whether or not the map I had with me showed a bridge by the building marked as Strathchailleach. Not knowing what the river would be like and whether or not I could ford it lower downstream I decided to head for the building where it at least looked narrower.

'By now the mist was right down and I was completely reliant on my compass. At Lochan nan Sac I contemplated turning round and heading back to my car. But I'm an optimist and I thought, given an hour or two, it would lift again. So I pressed on for Strathchailleach.

Enjoying the outdoor life – Sallie Tyszko

'I wasn't sure what I would find, but I thought there might be some shelter, if only an old barn where I could pause for a brew and a cigarette. I was amazed when I eventually spotted the cottage sitting right down in the bottom of the glen – there was smoke rising from the chimney. At that point I didn't think it likely anyone lived there. I thought it was more probable the fire belonged to hillwalkers, or maybe another angler.

'After tramping through a very damp bog, I reached the front door. I tried the latch and found the door was not locked, so I pushed it open. As I did so, a figure appeared inside. It was rather gloomy, but I could just make out a man with a dark beard and penetrating eyes. He was as surprised to see me, as I was to see him.

'He asked what I wanted and I explained I was out camping and fishing and was looking for a safe place to cross the river. At first he look none too welcoming, but to my surprise he stepped back from the door and invited me in.

'It was very dark and smoky inside the cottage. There wasn't much light coming through the tiny window and the fire in the grate was struggling to produce any flame, just lots of smoke, most of which was circulating in the room. My initial reaction was that this man had sought out the cottage for the same reason as me – for a bit of shelter. But, as I looked around, I started to wonder if he might actually live there.

'There wasn't much furniture – just a table and a couple of seats made from wooden boxes. But he appeared to be remarkably settled, as if it was in fact his home. I remember starting to feel slightly guilty that I had wandered in on him unannounced.

'He offered me a cup of tea and a seat by the fire. I remember thinking how muddled the place looked. There were piles of books and magazine and some newspapers too. Most of them looked old, damp, faded and rather crumpled. There were also small piles of paper, pages torn from magazines.

'Over tea and a packet of biscuits which I had with me in my rucksack, we got talking. Despite his isolation he seemed to be remarkably well informed on what was happening in the outside world. He said he read a lot, particularly in the evenings when it was too dark to go outside. I asked him how he got hold of all the books and magazines and he said most were left by visitors or given to him by people he knew in Kinlochbervie. All were read. Some he read again or kept articles or pictures from. Others ended up on the fire.

'He said he painted too and directed my attention to the ceiling which was mainly black. But he pointed out stars and planets and told me it was the night sky above the cottage. He said he spent many hours studying it on clear nights.'

Steve Moss left the cottage at Strathchailleach after accepting the offer of a dram of whisky to keep him going on his trek.

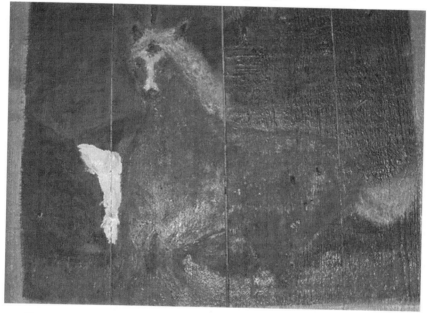

James McRory Smith's painting of a horse – James Carron

'I was amazed that someone would choose to live in such an isolated place. He seemed to be content and happy and there was no indication during our conversation that, even with very little, he wanted for anything. I remember, as I walked north, trying to comprehend how difficult it would be to live alone here, with only passing strangers for company. He obviously managed to keep his mind occupied reading and painting and, despite this reclusive lifestyle, he struck me as an intelligent and articulate man,' Steve added.

Although a regular point of contact in Kinlochbervie, friend Sallie Tyszko seldom visited James at Strathchailleach. But she too recalls how important reading was to him.

'I walked into the bothy a few times over the years,' she said. 'I always took with me food and sometimes things he needed to make repairs to the cottage. He never had much but people did leave him stuff. He was very keen on reading, particularly astrology and stories about pioneers. He had no way of getting books for himself so he relied on the generosity of others.'

To the casual observer, it is perhaps surprising that astrology figured among James' passions. He was known to be a very practical man, not a characteristic one would immediately associate with a subject regarded by many astronomers and scientists as little more than superstition.

'He was very interested in birth charts,' Sallie continued. 'I guess he must have taught himself how to read them. There is a lot to learn as they are very complicated but he knew exactly what he was doing. He did readings for other people, including myself. It was very detailed.'

From the dawn of time, man has gazed in wonder at the heavens above, seeking to understand the relationship between the sun, moon, planets and stars. The ancient Mesopotamians, Egyptians, and Greeks studied the movements they witnessed in the night sky and the calculations they recorded underpin the science of astronomy. Astrology – the study of heavenly bodies to learn what influence they may have on human life – is less precise and has long been the subject of much speculation and, from sections of the scientific community, derision. It has, however, enjoyed a popular following with many people all over the world consulting horoscopes on a daily basis in the belief their sun sign may foretell future events.

It is not known when James developed his interest in astrology. However, he clearly spent a lot of time at Strathchailleach studying the night sky, the proof of this taking physical form in the nightscape that adorned the ceiling of his living room. He not only painted the stars and planets he could see, but he also added astrological symbols, referred to by John Slater after his 1976 visit as 'strange squiggled letters'.

James' interest in astrology extended far beyond simply checking his own horoscope – he compiled his own Book of the Zodiac, a large bound volume that he concealed safely within the bothy. It was a treasured possession and one he devoted much time and energy to. Those who knew of this interest believe he drew what knowledge he could from the books and magazines he received from friends and visitors.

Much has been written on the subject of astrology and forecasts appear in the majority of newspapers and many popular magazines. An individual's astrological horoscope – or birth chart – is determined by the position of all the planets at the exact moment the person was born. Early astrologers divided the year into 12 equal portions, called the zodiac, which corresponded to 12 constellations lying in a great belt around the heavens. This was based on the concept that the sun passes through the 12 constellations of the zodiac during the course of a year.

Various paintings by James McRory Smith – James Carron

Each of the 12 sections was assigned a name and a symbol, based on animals, giving us the star signs we are familiar with today. Each constellation was regarded as the house of a particular planet, although some planets ruled more than one constellation. Each planet was believed to have either a strong or a weak influence on a person's life, depending on its position in the heavens. The 12 signs of the zodiac were also thought to have a relationship with parts of the human body and to the four classical Greek elements – earth, air, fire, and water.

From this, astrologers believe they can predict what may happen to a person. Aside from the daily horoscope forecasts published in newspapers, there are many people who consult more detailed birth charts for specific information that may influence decisions they subsequently take.

James developed the ability to conduct detailed horoscope readings of this nature and, using his cherished Zodiak book, he would predict what the stars held for others, sometimes at his bothy, sometimes at the public bar of the Garbet Hotel.

Bernard Heath enjoyed a long friendship with James and recalls his astrological readings in a short article originally published in the newsletter of the Mountain Bothies Association.

He wrote: 'James was into astrology and for a small fee he would ask a few questions such as birthday, family connections, etc. Then he would look into his large book of the Zodiak, an almanac that for years he kept hidden under his table top suspended on strings out of sight. It took time. Sandy had plenty of this and he would turn the pages back and forth commenting on planetary positions and alignment, whilst you would sip peaty tea from a tiny glass cup. Sometimes he would be inconclusive so you would need to call again at his bothy for a full future to be foretold.'

It is not known why James developed such a strong interest in astrology. Perhaps he was trying to make sense of his own life and the death of his wife. Perhaps the character traits defined by the sun sign under which he himself was born, Pisces, offer some explanation. Pisceans are said to be the natural mediums and mystics of the zodiac, capable of communicating their inner vision through either the arts or the sciences.

Astrology is by no means an exact science and the same can be said for mythology, another subject area that interested James. Again his studies centred on the books and magazines he collected. This newfound knowledge he incorporated into many of his paintings, with mythological figures gracing the wall of his bothy long after his departure.

He devoted his waking hours to more earthly pursuits too. He took a keen interest in the birds, animals and insects that inhabited the hills and moor around the bothy. Some he spotted while out on his travels, others he encountered closer to home.

Sallie Tyszko remembered James telling her of an otter that befriended him.

'He was very good with animals,' she said. 'He once told me about an otter that visited him. I think he fed it fish heads. On a couple of occasions he even managed to entice it into the cottage. Then it disappeared and never returned. Some time later, however, another otter visited and it stayed for a week. Again he fed it with left over pieces of fish.

'Birds also visited the bothy and he put out scraps for them. I remember him telling me he laid a trail for one of the birds and managed to lead it right into the bothy.'

Despite the remote location of Strathchailleach, James managed to keep himself busy, whether it was following the fortunes of the creatures he shared the landscape with, or undertaking daily chores like collecting water, cutting peat, gathering firewood or fishing for food.

When the weather was fine, he spent much of his time out of doors, roaming the hills and moor. More often than not he had no final destination in mind when he set off. He was happy to simply walk. Sometimes, however, he set out with purpose. There was the weekly supply run to Kinlochbervie and on other occasions, he would strike a course north to the lighthouse at Cape Wrath for a chat and a cup of tea with the keepers stationed there.

At night, and on days when bad weather confined him to the cottage, he filled his time reading, painting and studying subjects like astrology and mythology. Occasional visitors brought human company and there was always the constant companionship of his small battery-powered transistor radio to fall back on. He took it wherever he went, listening either to Radio 4 or football commentaries.

He may have spent much of his time alone at Strathchailleach, but there is plenty of evidence to indicate he was not averse to human contact. Unfortunately, however, this little seen social side to his character would bring with it problems, most of which related to alcohol.

James was a heavy drinker, as those who knew him and visitors to the bothy both testify. Some say he was an alcoholic. He drank both in the privacy of his own home and socially in Kinlochbervie.

James McRory Smith – Howard Patrick

Francis and Janet Whittington visited Strathchailleach in 1994 during a walking holiday in the area and met James as he was emerging from one of his lengthy drinking binges. She recorded the experience in her diary.

Janet wrote: 'After a swim at the beach at Sandwood we pushed on again and struck across the Parph, passing a lochan to bring us insight of the well-concealed bothy in the river valley. We could see a red corrugated iron roof with smoke rising. Coming near we saw a grey-bearded figure sitting in the doorway. Francis went up and spoke.

'He said he'd been there for 20 years. He told us he had just emerged from two days on the whisky. His ruddy face already revealed something of the sort.

'A couple of days later, we were chatting with Mrs MacLeod, owner of the bungalow in Sheigra we were staying in and she told us that Sandy had been a steel erector from Glasgow, but he had had a fall which made him peculiar with a tendency to the bottle.'

Alistair Currie, who visited Strathchailleach in the late 1960s added: 'He told me that he recognised he had some kind of drink problem and usually got into trouble when he walked over to Kinlochbervie to collect his social security money and therefore would try to avoid the local hotel in future. I don't know if he managed this.'

James' drinking did indeed land him in trouble. He frequently found himself barred from the public bars at the Garbet Hotel, in Kinlochleven, and the Rhiconich Hotel, four miles away, due to his behaviour while under the influence of alcohol. He was said to be boisterous and at times aggressive.

Sallie Tyszko remembers him as a happy drunk. 'Trouble often stemmed from drink,' she said. 'He was a happy drunk, there was no malice in him but he often got banned from the local bar. When new owners came in, he'd go back again, but he would soon be banned again.'

When James bought his provisions in Kinlochbervie, he would stock up on whisky and beer, as the following entry from the Strathchailleach bothy logbook confirms:

'In the early 1990s I would regularly pick up Sandy hitching between Kinlochbervie and the track. He always wanted me to take him along the track but I always refused. He was a cantankerous old bastard. But living here, carrying a rucksack and two carrier bags of messages (mainly beer) he had every right to be a wonderful character.'

James consumed so much whisky that he was able to use the empty bottles to mark the route from Blairmore to his remote home. According to Bernard Heath, the trail started at the Sandwood track gate and led all the way to the bothy.

'It was marked out with whisky bottles of all shapes and sizes and some can still be found to this day, every few hundred yards or so. They are all empties of course, scrupulously rinsed out with water, not a drop left. Many have been recycled and can be found serving as candleholders in the Cape Wrath bothies.'

Empty beer cans were simply left to rot within the walls of the ruined barn adjacent to the bothy, or were dumped in the room of the bothy that James did not use.

James McRory Smith's drink of choice – Howard Patrick

He also tried his hand at making his own beer, ordering a home brew kit and some say he created an illegal still, located in a hollow a short way upstream from Strathchailleach.

Bernard added: 'Sandy never quite mastered the distillation process, but he did send away and get a beer making kit and his bothy was at one time full of buckets, bowls and a flagon or two of some pretty foul smelling stuff.'

James' addiction to alcohol led not only to him being turned away from the bars of local hotels, but also resulted in him clashing with the local police force on a regular basis. His drunken behaviour resulted in him spending time in the cell at Rhiconoch Police Station on a number of occasions and although James bought much of the drink he consumed, there were times when he stole it, as a court report in the May 24, 1991, edition of the *Northern Times* confirms.

In February 1991, James broke into Bervie Stores in Kinlochbervie, smashing one of the windows and stealing three half bottles and a quarter bottle of whisky. He also took 10 packets of tobacco, a packet of cheese and a tub of margarine.

Police officers visited Strathchailleach where they recovered some of the items. At Dornoch Sheriff Court, James admitted the charges and was admonished. However, Sheriff Ewan Stewart ordered him to pay £250 compensation to the shop owner - £50 for the items taken and £200 to cover the damage to the window.

Over the years he was arrested on various occasions, mostly for breaches of the peace or thefts committed while under the influence of drink.

A serving Highland Constabulary officer, who did not wish to be identified, said: 'James was well known to the local police. He was not a dangerous man. He was more of a nuisance. Most of the incidents he was involved in were fairly petty and tended to be linked to alcohol.

'There were occasions when he stole from shops or unoccupied houses in the area, mainly holiday lets. He was an opportunist and would take things he needed, like food and drink or, where the opportunity arose, boots or clothing.

'Incidents were more prolific in the winter months and it is fair to say he was the most regular occupant of the cell at Rhiconoch Police Station.'

On many occasions, James was released the following morning with a warning after he had sobered up. However, there were times when his actions landed him in the dock at Dornoch Sheriff Court and, on at least one occasion, he served a period of incarceration at Portersfield Prison, in Inverness.

James' heavy drinking also resulted in potentially life-threatening situations. One frequently told tale relates to an incident, in the depths of winter, when James was heading home from a session at the Garbet Hotel bar, on one of the rare occasions when he was not barred. His nephew Andrew takes up the story.

'There are lots of tales about how tough he was,' Andrew said. 'One story that comes to mind took place in bitter cold winter weather. James was heading home from the pub when he fell over and collapsed on to the roadside verge. It was very cold and he quickly became frozen to the floor. He was there for some time before a passing shepherd found him. James was helped to his feet. He just dusted himself down and wandered off on his way.'

It is impossible to say when James turned to the bottle. He drank heavily throughout his time at Strathchaillech and continued to do so when he moved to Kinlochbervie, spending much of his money on drink. Indeed, he was drinking to such an extent that Ann Doull, one of the sales assistants at the Bervie Stores, would hold back some of his weekly pension to prevent him spending it all on alcohol.

From what Alistair Currie relates, James himself knew he had a problem but there is no evidence to suggest he ever sought any help to tackle it. Indeed, so self-reliant was he that he never once asked for any medical advice. While life at Strathchailleach may have, at times, been truly idyllic, James' drinking suggests he was not always happy in his own company, far less that of others. He may very well have been trying to block out difficult memories from the past, but he was soon to face a catastrophic event that would force him out of his beloved home and threaten the very future of his hard-fought existence.

*****

74

6

Life at Strathchailleach was lived at the mercy of the elements. In such a remote spot, the weather played a key role in dictating the day-to-day activities of James McRory Smith. Storms and blizzards could confine the recluse to his bothy home for days on end while heavy snowfall rendered the trek into Kinlochbervie for supplies an impossible task. He prepared as best he could. During the autumn he dug and stockpiled peat in the hope it would see him through the darkest days of winter.

For almost 20 years he survived the elements unscathed. Then, in the winter of early 1979, disaster struck. Late one night, James retired to his bed as normal. A storm was brewing outside, but as he pulled up his tattered blankets to ward off the cold, the last embers in the fire now dying in the blackened grate, he had no idea just how precarious his existence was.

Outside on the moor, the wind was gathering strength. Whipping off the Atlantic Ocean, potent gusts roared over the tin roof of the bothy. James had experienced storms in the past, on numerous occasions, and was probably not too concerned by this one. It was just another windy night in Strath Chailleach, and there were plenty of those over the years.

He drifted off to sleep, helped no doubt by the comforting caress of whisky ebbing through his veins. He slept soundly, oblivious to the deteriorating conditions outside. Then, in the dead of night, he was rudely awakened from his serene slumber by a catastrophic crashing sound. As he lay in his bed, he felt the whole cottage shudder and rumble.

James did not immediately investigate the cause of the crashing sound. He remained in his bed as it slowly subsided, listening intently for any further unwelcome intrusions. The room he occupied remained in tact, as did the roof above him and although the storm raged on outside, he was content to stay where he was, safely wrapped in his blankets.

The following morning, he rose early and prepared to set about his daily round of chores. But as he stepped out he noticed something was seriously amiss. There was a large hole in the western gable of the cottage. Although the roof and part of the chimney remained, much of the wall had fallen in, scattering rubble and debris through the western room. He rarely used this part of the bothy, but he would have been well aware that, without the gable, another storm could easily tear the roof off the whole cottage. It was a major catastrophe for him.

James had limited building experience. He undertook minor repairs and maintenance work at Strathchailleach, but he was now faced with the task of rebuilding a complete section of wall. He did not have the tools or materials for such a big job. And the fallen gable was not the only work required. Despite his best efforts, the little cottage was in a poor state.

Faced with the prospect of losing his roof, James packed a few possessions and moved out. With nowhere to go and no one to turn to, he returned to his itinerant ways. He told no one of his departure and simply disappeared.

In Kinlochbervie, enquiries were made after James failed to turn up at the Post Office in Balchrick to collect his social security money. A police officer was despatched to the bothy but he returned with the news that there was no sign of him. Over time, it was assumed James had died, perhaps out on the moor, and the June 1981 issue of the MBA Newsletter records that in June 1980, Bernard Heath and his wife Betty heard from local police that he had not been seen for some 18 months.

The couple visited the bothy to assess the damage. They found the cottage in 'poor shape'. Although the roof remained on, with the hole in the gable it was completely at the mercy of the wind.

The MBA had long held an interest in Strathchailleach. Bernard Heath first visited in 1955, when he discovered the cottage as he cycled north to Cape Wrath. A keen walker and cyclist, he identified it as a possible bothy, a refuge for people travelling through this remote part of Scotland.

Bernard's passion for the outdoors and staying in bothies led, in 1965, to the formation of the MBA. Bothies had been around for many years and the word bothy comes from the Gaelic term bothan – a hut. Most were remote cottages, built originally for shepherds or estate workers. Over time, their occupants abandoned them as the arrival of new technology, particularly the Land Rover, made it easier to access the remoter corners of the Scottish countryside, removing the need to have someone live there permanently.

After the Second World War, economic growth led to an increase in the popularity of outdoor pursuits such as hillwalking and mountaineering and these empty cottages found a new use, offering shelter to walkers and climbers. Some were adopted by climbing clubs while others were used either clandestinely or with the approval of the landowner. Over time, the term 'bothying' was coined to describe the use of such remote cottages and huts.

Increased popularity brought with it problems. While some bothies were fortunate enough to enjoy the financial support of climbing clubs or groups of enthusiastic individuals, the majority were not and many quickly deteriorated. In 1965, steps were taken to address this situation and on December 28 of that year the MBA held its inaugural meeting. The first committee was formed and in January 1966 the MBA published its first newsletter. In the early days, one of the main priorities was to identify potential bothies and the help of members was enlisted in this task. The first list identified 100 possible candidates and over time this steadily grew.

MBA members demonstrated what they could do at Tunskeen, in the Galloway Hills, where a ruined farmhouse was renovated into a basic shelter. It was the MBA's first bothy and other projects followed, all consistent with the association's simple aim 'to maintain simply shelters in remote country for the use and benefit of all who love wild and lonely places'.

Although Bernard Heath identified Strathchailleach as a possible MBA bothy in 1955, when he returned some years later with a view to taking the project forward, he found James McRory Smith in residence and the association turned its attention instead to nearby Strathan, which was renovated over six days in 1976.

The MBA was not alone in spotting Strathchailleach's potential as a shelter. In 1977, Ian Mackenzie, of Perth, published *A Survey of Shelters in Remote Mountain Areas of the Scottish Highlands*. The study identified and briefly described around 400 buildings that might provide shelter in remote areas. Each entry included location, access information and an account of the building. Strathchailleach was surveyed in 1974.

The entry read: 'A Land Rover track crosses the moors to Loch a' Mhuilinn and thence there is a moorland footpath to Sandwood Bay. Beyond Sandwood Bay there is a path via Lochan nan Sac to Strathchailleach but this is indistinct in parts. The bothy is very low and appears to be hidden in the south bank of the Strath Chailleach river. A small low walled stone cottage with a corrugated iron roof. Inhabited by a recluse who has been squatting here for some eight years. Shelter may be offered but this will be subject to the resident's benevolence.'

The study also revealed the condition of Sandwood Lodge in 1974. For many years both before and after this date visitors to the beach used it as a makeshift bothy.

Bernard and Betty Heath at Strathchailleach – James Carron

The survey found: 'A stone-built house with corrugated iron roof. The upper floor is completely away and the upper floor beams are missing. There are no doors or windows. The windows are blocked with peat blocks. The floor is earth. There is a fireplace but only driftwood locally for fuel. There appears to have been undue use and consequent vandalism.'

Despite not being able to take Strathchailleach forward as a bothy project, Bernard and Betty Heath kept a close eye on the cottage and, over the years, developed a friendship with the reclusive occupant.

After their visit to the dilapidated cottage in 1980, the MBA decided the time had at last come to take Strathchailleach in hand. Plans were drawn up to renovate the building and permission was sought from the Keoldale Estate.

The December 1980 MBA Journal reported that definite permission had been received from the estate and outlined the work required: 'Rebuilding one gable end, repainting the roof and internal repairs are the order of the day at Strathchailleach.'

Concern remained, however, about James' interest in the bothy, particularly when it was revealed that he was not in fact dead, as had been thought.

Word filtered back to the MBA that he had spent some time, possibly as long as three or four months, squatting at Gorton bothy, a place he was familiar with from his previous stay when he was working at Rannoch Forest.

His other movements during the 18 months or so that he was away from Strathchailleach remain a mystery. What is known, however, is that he returned briefly to the Kinlochbervie area only to be arrested. At Dornoch Sheriff Court he was sentenced to three months in Portersfield Prison, in Inverness, following a series of breaches of the peace committed while under the influence of alcohol.

There he managed to broker an unusual and rather audacious deal with Bernard and Betty Heath and the MBA that would enable him to return to a renovated Strathchailleach.

According to Bernard Heath, within the uneasy confines of the prison visitors' room, James renewed his efforts for MBA support to repair the cottage.

'The west room, which had always been full of foul rubbish, floorless and often flooded, and now even worse with no gable wall, was to become, after major repairs, the open MBA bothy room. Sandy would have sole use of the best room with its open fire and his wee back bedroom as before,' Bernard said.

In January 1981, the MBA agreed to proceed with the project on this basis, fearing that without intervention the cottage may be lost forever. A major work party was scheduled for Easter 1981 and this proceeded as planned.

For its renovation projects, the MBA relies on a volunteer workforce drawn from its own membership. One of the biggest challenges they faced at Strathchailleach was the remoteness of the location and the difficulties this presented in transporting building materials and other supplies to the site. A report on the work party, written by Bernard Heath and published in the MBA Newsletter of June 1981, reveals just how difficult this job was.

Although some of the MBA's more remote projects undertaken in later years utilised helicopter airlifts, this was not the case at Strathchailleach. All materials were transported overland, using a small all-terrain vehicle and much brute strength on the part of the small band of dedicated volunteers who attended.

On the first day of the project – April 17 – the party gathered at the start of the path to Sandwood Bay. Sacks of cement, wooden joists and other construction materials were loaded on to an Argocat, a small four-wheel drive vehicle commonly utilised by estates for transport over rough, often trackless ground.

Bernard wrote: 'The last knot was tied and the vehicle took off at a furious pace. Lurching off the track, it hurtled down a bank on to the moor, snarled and squirmed its way across a soggy ditch and the sped off towards Sandwood Bay. We never saw it again, but the vanguard of the party, who had set off for the bothy ahead of us, encountered it at the far end of Sandwood Bay. Here, on the steep slope above the outflow of Sandwood Loch sat the nine bags of cement accompanied by one Argocat wheel.'

Despite losing the use of the Argocat, the volunteers eventually managed to carry all the supplies in and, on arrival at Strathchailleach, found James back in residence. The cottage, however, was now in an even sorrier state than when Bernard and Betty Heath visited in 1980.

'We had expected to find a hole in the west gable wall which, with luck, might be repaired quickly. Instead of that we discovered to our dismay that the entire gable had collapsed leaving only the chimney stack still miraculously in position hanging over thin air,' Bernard added.

Using stone from the ruined barn adjacent to the west gable and rocks prized from the riverbed, the wall was reconstructed. Although it originally featured a fireplace and chimney, this was not rebuilt, but a window was instead incorporated into the new gable. Other repairs were made to the fabric of the building and the chimney above the main room used by James was re-pointed.

According to the report, James took an active role in the work with Bernard noting: 'In terms of physical energy, his contribution was probably heavier than anyone's.'

The first phase of the project was complete by April 27 when the volunteers left the site. They returned a few months later, in July, to lay a concrete floor and construct a sleeping platform in the west room, the one that would now be available for use by visitors and a sign was erected. It read: 'Left for the bothy-room, right for the private room'.

With the work done, Strathchailleach at last took its place on the MBA's maintenance list of bothies. The December 1981 MBA Journal noted that despite the two work parties not being as well attended as expected, the distance doubtless playing a part in that, a 'fine wee bothy did result'.

An update in the June 1981 Newsletter was less optimistic in its conclusion, offering perhaps a hint of what was to come.

It noted: 'So for the time being the MBA is sharing Strathchailleach Cottage with Sandy. While he has never caused trouble at Strathchailleach, please let us know if any problems arise from this arrangement.'

Problems would indeed arise from the arrangement and it was not long before worrying reports started to filter through to the MBA hierarchy. Within a few months of the renovation the MBA receive letters and telephone calls from members who had been denied access to Strathchailleach. All of the reports received indicated that James had reneged on his word.

Some visitors found the door locked while James himself turned others away.

Hillwalker Matt Dawson and two friends planned to spend the night at Strathchailleach in the summer of 1983.

'We were not aware of any problems before we set off for the bothy. We were not MBA members but we had heard of the bothy and knew the history behind it. We knew that an old hermit occupied two of the rooms but he was happy enough for visitors to stay in the third,' Matt explained.

'We arrived at the bothy to find the hermit sitting on the doorstep. It was a beautiful day and he appeared to be enjoying the sunshine. He was quite chatty at first but when we mentioned in conversation that we planned to stay over before heading on to Cape Wrath the next day he told us it was his home and not a bothy. We were quite surprised, as we genuinely believed it was an open bothy. But he was adamant. He told us the nearest bothy was at Strathan and he offered directions. He also said there was another, at Kervaig, where we could stay.

'It was too nice a day to waste time arguing with this old man so we walked off. Fortunately we had a tent with us. If we hadn't we would have been stuck. It was very disappointing.'

Some encounters with James were more extreme. In one incident, police charged James with breaching the peace after he returned to the bothy to find a group of hillwalkers sifting through his possessions. Believing they had eaten some of his food, he threatened them. They left, the police were called and James was apprehended but the charges were later dropped.

An uneasy couple of years followed as the MBA attempted to resolve the situation. Members planning trips to the area were warned of the possibility they may not be able to use the bothy and efforts were made to negotiate a solution with James.

It is hard to say exactly why James went back on his word. Prior to the renovation, there is no evidence to indicate he refused hillwalkers or anglers entry and there are those already mentioned who found hospitality rather than hostility at Strathchailleach.

It is possible that following its addition to the MBA maintenance list, visitor numbers to Strathchailleach rose. There was certainly an increase in visitor numbers to the area in the 1980s, particularly after the opening of the Kylesku Bridge on August 8, 1984, which enabled people to drive north from Ullapool without having to face the delays so often associated with the ferry it replaced.

The Third Statistical Account of Scotland, published in 1988, supports this. It states: 'There is firm evidence from Durness that the bridge has increased tourist traffic, with a substantial number of tourists claiming that they had been attracted by its presence. It is probable that tourism in Kinlochbervie has increased for the same reason.'

A lot of these new visitors were drawn to the area by the scenic beauty of Sandwood Bay and it is likely many explored further, walking north to Cape Wrath.

Although the MBA has long resisted publication of bothy locations and grid references, it does issue to its members a list of bothies in its care, and the list contains this information. This may have prompted more people to visit the cottage after 1981. User numbers are not recorded, so it is not possible to say if this happened but while James may have been able to cope with the occasional walker who passed his door prior to this time, he may not have anticipated a surge in visitors. Any increase would undoubtedly cause anxiety to a man who had originally sought the place out for the solitude it offered.

It is worth remembering that James was an alcoholic and drank heavily. Anecdotal evidence suggests that his reaction to visitors was often influenced by the amount he had consumed. The more alcohol he drank the less welcoming he apparently became.

There are other factors to consider too. James had experienced problems over the years with outdoor activity groups operating in the area, particularly wilderness survival courses aimed at testing businessmen and women. These were an increasingly common activity in the 1980s, particularly in this part of Scotland. The wild terrain was seen as a perfect testing ground for executives who were pushed to the limits of both physical and mental endurance in this rugged and unforgiving environment.

On more than one occasion, James found himself in conflict with these groups, as a conversation with Francis and Janet Whittington, who visited the bothy in 1994, revealed.

'He said that they were a menace, wrecking the bothy and the bridge at Strathan. They had also set fire to one of his peat stacks,' Janet recorded in her diary.

There were other incidents too where survival course groups, struggling to live on meagre rations and with no shelter, ransacked Strathchailleach, taking his food and drink.

This may have been one of the reasons why the reclusive James, a strong individual, appears to have had little time for official associations or authority figures attempting to influence his life, even if he did seek their help in times of crisis.

Sallie Tyzsko recalled: 'He didn't like any type of organisational body. He considered Strathchailleach to be his home as he was there first. The MBA did renovate the cottage and helped to maintain it. He needed them but at the same time, as far as he was concerned, it was his home.'

There are those who believe James hoodwinked the MBA into carrying out the renovation and made a promise he had no intention of honouring. There is no doubt the MBA is the only organisation that would have undertaken such a task. It is unlikely that the Keoldale Estate would have invested in a property they had no use for and James himself did not have the funds or the resources necessary to undertake the repairs.

As a homeless person, the local council would have been obliged to re-house him, but it would certainly not have considered rebuilding Strathchailleach. The authority would have offered him a house in Kinlochbervie. It is highly unlikely James would have even contemplated such a move.

It is fair to say that if James wanted to return to the bothy he called home, he had no option but to seek the help of the MBA. But his failure to abide by his side of the agreement soured the relationship between the two parties and tarnished James' reputation with many in the hill-going community. It left a lasting impression on the association's membership. Some still resent his unwillingness to admit visitors to the bothy after the renovation, while others accept that he had the right to call the place home after living there for so long.

Having weathering the devastating tempest of 1979, James found himself at the centre of a storm of controversy. But with the bothy he called home wind and watertight once more, he dug his heels in. With no amicable settlement on the horizon, the MBA, which had spent a considerable sum of money on the repair work, was forced to admit defeat. In 1984 Strathchailleach was dropped from the maintenance list.

While bothy users were discouraged from visiting Strathchailleach, the growth of tourism in the north of Scotland was drawing more and more people to Sandwood. For many years, James shared the bay with only occasional visitors, mainly hillwalkers and anglers. Now he would have to deal with an influx of holidaymakers. This brought both problems, and opportunities.

*****

7

The 1980s saw a period of great change for the people of Kinlochbervie. Tourism was booming following the opening of the Kylesku Bridge and the local fishing industry was delivering big dividends after years of investment in the port. In 1984, annual fish landings passed through the £10 million mark for the first time ever. Kinlochbervie was now the third largest fishing harbour in Scotland, after Peterhead and Aberdeen. The years of slow decline were over. The community was a busy, prosperous place enjoying all the trappings of success.

The village would not, however, rest on its laurels. In January 1985 proposals were drawn up for a new fish market designed to serve larger trawlers. The number of lorries arriving and leaving each day increased too, helped on their way not by the bridge at Kylesku, but by improvements to the A9 trunk road linking Inverness with Perth. Upgrades on this vital route to the Highlands cut the time it took to transport fish to markets in the south, with many old bottlenecks bypassed.

There was investment too in industrial units, built at the harbour to encourage new businesses, plus new houses, education and health services. The mains water system, so long a problem for householders in the village and surrounding area, was also renewed.

Economic growth halted the trend of depopulation, a factor that had long been a problem. In 1984, the census revealed there were 436 people living in the village, a substantial increase in the 1971 figure of 344. The majority of those in work were employed in fishing, but there were a significant number of jobs in tourism-related businesses, like hotels. And there were employment opportunities not just for natives, but also for incoming families.

The future of Kinlochbervie no longer lay in the traditional industries of crofting and farming. It lay in fishing and tourism and there was talk too of an oil boom, with hopes pinned on reserves in the Minch.

Of course, the development of the fishing industry and the construction of new houses in Kinlochbervie mattered little to James McRory Smith who continued to live in blissful isolation at Strathchailleach. Doubtless he would have witnessed new faces on his weekly trips into the village. He would have seen the increase in traffic through the harbour and spotted build work proceeding apace as he wandered the streets clutching his plastic bags of messages.

Tourism would have the most significant impact on his way of life, thanks mainly to the growing popularity of Sandwood Bay, one of the region's most scenic natural attractions. For decades this strip of golden sand bounded at each end by high cliffs was a well-kept secret, known only to those prepared to venture off the beaten track. However, as visitor numbers to the area grew, word spread of this magnificent spot and more and more people made the trek in.

The bay can only be reached on foot, a feature that has prevented development from encroaching upon this sacred spot. It boasts some of the finest coastal scenery, not just in Scotland but also in Europe. Between Sandwood and Sheigra the cliffs rise to over 90 metres in height and at the southern end of the bay there is a 60-metre high sea stack, Am Buachaille. Inland, behind a complex system of dunes, Sandwood Loch cuts a rippling swathe through the landscape.

It was a place James new well. The beach was just a mile and a half as the crow flies from his front door and he regularly trod the sand, collecting driftwood washed up by the rolling Atlantic breakers. He spent many hours exploring the seashore and its hinterland. His enthusiasm for the area's flora and fauna was rewarded with sightings of seabirds like fulmar, puffins, kittiwakes, shags and guillemots, all of which thrive in the maritime cliff habitats on this wild stretch of coast.

There were nights when James would swap the relative comfort of Strathchailleach for Sandwood Lodge. Overlooking Sandwood Loch, the house originally provided accommodation for well-to-do Victorian and Edwardian travellers, drawn to the area by the lure of hunting, shooting and fishing. Later shepherds tending the estate flocks occupied the remote outpost before, like Strathchailleach, it was abandoned to the elements and left to decay. Despite the onset of dereliction, the crumbling cottage served as a less than salubrious bothy well into the 1980s. When the John Muir Trust bought the estate, the ruins were stabilised but there are no plans to reconstruct the building.

Sandwood is not just a place of great beauty; it also has strong links with the supernatural. There are many mysterious and ghostly tales associated with the bay and its hinterland. Some probably owe their existence to the area's remarkable isolation while others are rooted in actual events, some of which are equally puzzling and have yet to be fully resolved. There are those who believe James McRory-Smith contributed, perhaps unknowingly, to the propagation of paranormal stories.

Sightings of mermaids have been numerous and reports were made as late as the start of the 20th century. A local farmer, Alexander Gunn, made one of the best-documented sightings on January 5, 1900. Gunn was walking on the beach with his collie when the dog is said to have let out a howl and then retreated to his feet where it cringed in terror.

On a ledge above the sand Gunn claimed he saw a figure reclining on the rock. Initially he thought it was a seal, but on closer examination he saw the apparition had reddish-yellow hair, greenish blue eyes and a yellow body about seven feet in length.

Gunn died in 1944 but over the intervening years his story never changed and he maintained that he had seen a 'mermaid of ravishing beauty'.

Historically, mermaids of the type Gunn claimed to have seen were said to lure seafarers on to the rocks and scores of ships have run aground or been wrecked at Sandwood over the centuries.

In the 1920s, author Seton Gordon visited the bay as part of research that led, in 1935, to the publication of his classic travel book *Highways & Byways in the West Highlands*. He witnessed many submerged wrecks on the beach at Sandwood and wrote: 'I was astonished at the number of wrecks which lie on the fine sand of this bay. All of them are old tragedies: since the placing of a lighthouse on Cape Wrath just over a hundred years ago, no vessel has been lost here. Some of the vessels lie almost buried in the sand far above the reach of the highest tide'.

Seton paints a picture of a bay littered with wrecks and it is thought many more languish on the seabed offshore. Contrary to his statement that no ships sank here after the opening of the lighthouse at Cape Wrath in 1828, loses did continue and archaeological records held by Highland Council reveal details of just a few. They illustrate how treacherous the waters off the bay are, even without the interference of mermaids.

On October 24, 1845, an Inverness-based schooner loaded with wool ran aground at Sandwood. The ship's master and one of his crew drowned in the accident but the boat was subsequently refloated and continued on its voyage.

The following year, on April 11, the *Northumberland*, en route from South Shields to Newfoundland, was driven on to the beach by rolling seas and high winds. The Marine List recorded no loss of life with the whole crew being saved. Again the boat was rescued and put to sea again.

The *Three Brothers*, a brig from Ardrossan, was less fortunate. She ran aground on the beach on December 20, 1858, and, although the crew was saved, the 138-ton Irvine-registered vessel, which was carrying 'deals and spars', was wrecked.

Just days after the loss of the *Three Brothers*, another ship suffered a similar fate. The 100-ton Cork-registered *Minerva* was abandoned by her crew off the Butt of Lewis and the boat, laden with tar, was swept east by the currents. On December 29 she was thrown on to rocks at Sandwood and smashed to pieces.

On September 18, 1885, a fishing boat named *Aid*, sailing from Lerwick to Belfast, ran into difficulties as she traversed the bay. Floundering in high winds, she was blown ashore and wrecked

Mercifully, the majority of the men aboard these stricken vessels were saved. Many others were less fortunate, particularly during the first and second world wars when vessel travelling through the Minch found themselves coming under attack from German submarines and aircraft.

The proliferation of wrecks and the many lives lost in this remote spot have fuelled various supernatural stories. One of Sandwood Bay's most famous and enduring ghosts is linked to a shipwreck, a

Polish vessel said to have sunk in the bay. Sporting a dark beard and clad in sea boots, a sailor's cap and a brass buttoned tunic the spectre has, over the years, been witnessed wandering the beach by crofters, fishermen and walkers.

There have been reports too of a ghost at Sandwood Lodge, a spirit who makes its presence felt through the sound of heavy footsteps. It is possible that this ghost and the bearded sailor are one in the same.

Another story tells of a group of three local men who were returning to Blairmore from Sandwood Bay. As they left the beach one of the men suddenly felt something drop on his toe. Initially he accused his companions of stepping on his foot or dropping something on it. However, neither of the other two men was close enough at the time to have done this.

A week later the men returned to the bay to recover the body of a sailor washed ashore. They collected the dead man's remains in a coffin and set off for home. However, at exactly the same spot where the man had a week earlier felt something jabbing at his foot, the coffin dropped on his toe. Was this an eerie premonition, or simply coincidence? No one will ever know.

Whether or not one holds store in tales of supernatural activity, there are those who believe James McRory Smith may have been responsible for some of the sightings of the bearded sailor. He visited the beach regularly, sported a heavy beard that was, in the 1960s and 70s at least, black in colour, and dressed in attire that could easily be mistaken for that of a mariner.

In the obituary to James in *Am Bratach*, the author states: 'Sandwood Bay is the possessor of the ghost of a sea captain and I feel sure that James with his peaked cap, bushy beard and navy jacket could have easily been mistaken for him as he made his way home in the gloaming.'

Mountain Bothies Association stalwart Bernard Heath is of a similar mind and, in the text of a memorial plaque erected in Strathchailleach following James' death, he wrote: 'Over the recent years Sandy was, I believe, the living ghost seen by many in the bay of Sandwood.'

He said: 'For centuries there have been stories about Sandwood ghosts. The favourite ones involve people sighting an old sailor, short in stature, heavily bearded, usually carrying a sack on his shoulder.'

Bernard believes some of the 'ghost' sightings stem from people seeing James on the beach while others, who approached the ghostly figure, were surprised to discover he was not a supernatural apparition but a very real person.

'Some people got a fright. They had heard tell of the ghost of the shipwrecked mariner, but there he was in the flesh,' he added.

Sandwood may have its ghosts, but there are other mysteries too, such as where the remains of a wartime aircraft now lie. On September 30, 1941 the pilot of an RAF Spitfire was forced to make an emergency landing on the beach after his engine cut out. It must have been a particularly skilful landing as the pilot managed to put down on the beach, missing the cliffs at either end of the bay, the sea and Sandwood Loch. He escaped unhurt and was taken to the house of a local shepherd where he was given tea ahead of his return to base. As was the case with most air crashes during the Second World War, the wreckage was never recovered. The plane was slowly consumed by the shifting sands and disappeared completely. Over the years efforts have been made to locate the wreckage and, from time to time, the Spitfire reveals itself briefly, only to disappear once again.

Shipwrecks and wartime aircraft are not the only objects concealed beneath the sand. Human remains have been uncovered too. In 1986 a visitor to the beach found bones in the dunes and a subsequent excavation uncovered the skeletons of an adult and a child. These were taken to Raigmore Hospital in Inverness for pathological examination and were found to be over 100 years old.

In 1992, Herbert Shearer, on holiday from Aberfeldy, found another human skeleton, this time on a shelf above the beach at the north end of the bay. Again the bones were examined at Raigmore Hospital and they were found to be between 100 and 150 years old. A report on the find appeared in the Press & Journal of July 6, 1992, under the gloriously gory headline: 'Skeleton mystery at bay of ghosts'.

It stated: 'Police believe the remains are possibly from early this century – a sailor washed ashore during World War I, or part of an old burial ground uncovered by wind and wave action'.

As a regular visitor to the beach, James McRory Smith would doubtless have witnessed some unusual sights during his many years at Strathchailleach. The winter months in particular saw massive movements in the sand, caused by strong winds and ferocious seas. The dunes at Sandwood are among the most dynamic in the British Isles. He may very well have seen the remains of wrecked ships, or indeed caught a glimpse of the illusive Spitfire.

The shifting sands threw up wood for his fire, fish and fruit boxes, rope, tarpaulins and other items he could utilise back at the bothy. James was a skilled beachcomber, but he was also adept at tapping unwary visitors to the bay.

Bernard Heath relates a story that highlights just how inventive he could be, albeit to fraudulently obtain money.

'One day Sandy headed out across the Sandwood shores for his weekly supplies,' Bernard said. 'It was worth noting that he must have met from time to time solo walkers claiming sponsorship and raising money for some charitable good cause.

'This day he had a bright idea. On finding a small tent at Sandwood he called out cheerily. Two youths appeared. Sandy explained that he was on a walk to raise funds for the local seaman's mission. The boys were moved to part with a fiver each. Later Sandy was seen standing his hand – a rare event – at the Garbet Bar.'

There were occasions too when he scrounged food and drink from campers pitched amongst the dunes, or staying at the Sandwood House bothy. In the late 1970s, Barry Abbot and three friends visited Sandwood Bay with the intention of climbing in the area. They based themselves at the bothy and, on their first day out, spent time exploring the beach and cliffs.

'Late in the day, as we headed back to the bothy, we saw a strange bearded figure walking on the beach. He was some way off. We had all heard the story of the ancient mariner said to haunt Sandwood and, to be honest, I felt a bit uneasy. None of us believed in ghosts, but this was quite spooky,' Barry recalled.

'The figure was walking towards us and it soon became clear this was no ghost, but an old guy. He was wearing a long oilskin jacket over a blue boiler suit. The trouser legs were rolled up to his knees and he was barefoot. I remember he had a very ruddy face, black hair and a dark beard which was greying a little around his chin.

'We started chatting. He didn't say much about himself but he seemed to be very interested in what we were doing. He was friendly enough, so, in conversation, we told him we were staying up at the bothy, which in those days had a roof. He told us he lived in a cottage to the north of the bay.

'I remember him asking if we had any cigarettes. I offered him my pack, but rather than just take one he took three. Then he wandered off along the beach. We thought that was the last we would hear of him. We finished our day on the beach gathering driftwood and headed back up to the bothy for supper.

'Later that night, as we sat round a roaring fire, the old man appeared out of the dark at the door of the bothy. He was clutching a metal tin. We cleared a seat by the fire for him and he sat down. The tin, it soon turned out, contained home brew. He offered it round and we took some. It tasted awful. In return we plied him with whisky and fags.

'It is hard to remember exactly what we talked about, as we were all drinking quite heavily. But I remember being surprised that this rather rough and ready looking man, who told us his name was Sandy McRory, was knowledgeable about books and literature and, despite living in such an isolated spot, he was well up on current affairs and sport.

'He became a regular fixture around our bothy fires during our stay at Sandwood, always appearing late and then disappearing off into the night when the whisky ran out. He told us lots of stories about the area, but very little about himself. We suggested a visit to his cottage, but he seemed keener to drop in on us and we never made it as far as Strathchailleach.

'When the time came to leave Sandwood and head for home, we wondered if Sandy would appear to see us off. But there was no sign of him and we left without saying goodbye. We did, however, leave behind half a bottle of whisky and some cigarettes which I have no doubt he would have found and appreciated.'

While James was able to discourage some, like Barry and his climbing companions, from straying from the bay towards his remote idyll, others would call at his door and not all were so easily deterred.

*****

7

There was no gas, electricity or telephone at Strathchailleach and with no rent or rates to pay James McRory Smith never had to worry about bills. He could spend his money as he saw fit, on food, cigarettes and alcohol. In the Spring of 1989, however, he was in for a rude awakening.

Arriving at Balchrick Post Office to pick up his pension, he found himself in receipt of a letter. James very rarely received mail. What letters did make their way to him were held for his collection at the Post Office, saving the Royal Mail a lengthy hike to Strathchailleach. This particular letter arrived in an official looking envelope. It was a demand for money, from Highland Regional Council. James joined his fellow Scots in receipt of their first Community Charge bills.

The Community Charge – or poll tax as it was more commonly know – was introduced in April 1989 by Margaret Thatcher's Conservative government. Launched in Scotland a full year ahead of its introduction in England, it was a fixed tax levied on all households in the country and replaced the old rates system which had taxed people according to the value of the property they owned.

Under the new system, every person would pay for the community services they used. Many believed it was an attempt to shift the tax burden from the rich to the poor. As a result, there was significant opposition to the concept and this increased as the financial demands issued by local authorities to their residents proved to be considerably higher than initially predicted.

Resistance quickly led to hostility and campaigns of mass non-payment were initiated, leading to angry public demonstrations. In some areas, as many as a third of former ratepayers defaulted and while owner-occupiers were easy to tax, those who frequently changed addresses were more difficult pursue. The cost of collecting the community charge rose steeply while returns fell and enforcement measures became increasingly draconian leading, in some areas, to riots.

James received his demand for payment, despite the fact he lived in a property located miles from anywhere and with no basic services. Income from the community charge paid for council services such as roads and pavements, street lighting, rubbish collection, education and social work and leisure facilities. It also funded the provision of mains water and drainage. Strathchailleach was many miles from the nearest road. There was no public water or drainage connection and no rubbish collection. James did not benefit from education and social work services and never utilised local authority leisure amenities. Perhaps not surprisingly, he had no intention of paying this new tax.

Sallie Tyszko said: 'I was astonished that given where James lived, he was charged for the poll tax. The council sent him a demand. He was aghast at that.'

Sallie found herself in a similar position. Living in a very basic cottage in Kinlochbervie she too resisted payment. What became of the first community charge bill sent to Strathchailleach is unknown. It is safe to assume, however, that it probably ended up in the fire.

'We were both in the same boat,' Sallie continued. 'I had no intention of paying as the cottage I live in was without many of the basic services. James had even less, living at Strathchailleach. He had never had to pay a bill in all the time he lived there and, as far as he was concerned, he had no intention of starting now.'

But matters did not end there. The council, faced with increasing levels of non-payment, had issued the demand and would follow it up in the same way as they did other arrears. Unfortunately for them, James was no ordinary resident and it quickly became clear that administering this debt would be no walk in the park. When people defaulted on their payments, the local authority had a number of means of collection at their disposal. These included making deductions from wages or freezing bank accounts. James had neither a wage nor a bank account. The next step was to instruct bailiffs to seize a defaulter's goods, selling them at auction to recover the debt. James had very few possessions and none of them held any fiscal value.

'I remember at one stage two men actually walked out to the bothy,' Sallie continued. 'They had obviously been sent to take whatever they could to meet the bill. But they returned empty handed. There was nothing of any value there.'

Highland Regional Council was forced to cut its losses. With no hope of receiving any payment, they let the matter drop, deciding against dragging the recluse through the courts.

With their demand letters now embers in his fire, James returned to his bill-free way of life. For Margaret Thatcher, the universally unpopular poll tax signalled the end of her reign as Prime Minister and her successor, John Major, replaced it with the Council Tax in 1993.

In its short life, the poll tax was rarely out of the headlines and James' battle with officialdom also attracted media attention. Although he personally never courted such interest, a journalist picked up on the story and his subsequent report was to answer the key question praying on the minds of James' family back in Dumbarton – what had become of him?

Other than a few Christmas cards sent in the years after he left home to join the army there had been no contact and relatives did not know where he was, or indeed if he was even still alive. Then, in the autumn of 1992, there was a sudden revelation, delivered through the pages of a tabloid newspaper.

Nephew Andrew Smith recalls the moment he opened his newspaper over breakfast and spotted a familiar face.

'I was working in Eastbourne at the time and I used to get the *Sunday Mail* there. One Sunday I was reading through the paper when I saw a photo of my uncle,' he said.

The date was October 11, 1992, and, on page three under the headline 'Take a Hike Jimmy!' there was a photograph of James McRory Smith, resplendent in his white beard and flat cap.

The accompanying story, subtitled 'OAP's 26-mile trek for pension,' told of the round trip James made come 'hail, rain or shine' to collect his pension at the Balchrick Post Office and then buy supplies in Kinlochbervie. He was branded 'Scotland's hardiest pensioner'.

'I often wondered what happened to Uncle James but we never heard anything from him or about him,' Andrew continued. 'We knew he was a bit of a wanderer but we had no idea where he ended up. We didn't even know if he was still alive, so this came right out of the blue.'

Relatives in Dumbarton and elsewhere in Britain were soon on the telephone, contacting each other, urging one another to buy a copy of the paper to read the story.

James' niece Ella Connolly said, 'As soon as I saw the picture I knew it was James. He looked so like his brother Billy, even with the beard.'

A few days before the story appeared journalist Jim Lawson trekked into the bothy to interview James. It was one of the more unusual assignments he had covered for the paper.

'He came to our attention from reports about the council trying to get the poll tax off him. If I remember right, there was a court case and they sent a bailiff to collect the money. He had to walk into the bothy,' the reporter said.

'We decided to follow the story up and myself and a photographer walked to the bothy. It started out okay but it got very wet and when we arrived at the bothy we found one of the rooms was flooded.'

In the curious setting of a waterlogged cottage, Jim Lawson interviewed James and, after making the long walk back to civilisation, filed his copy to the *Sunday Mail* news desk in Glasgow. The resulting story featured James' own words, the first and only time they have ever appeared in print. The article offers a brief insight to his life at the bothy at the time and his reasons for living there.

On his decision to move to such a remote spot, he is quoted as saying: 'I enjoy a simple life. I moved to this area over 20 years ago when I decided to drop out of the rat race. Now my life is perfect and I would like to stay here forever.

'Walking keeps me healthy and I reckon I've trekked thousands of miles to collect my pension and my messages. The only trouble is that I keep wearing out my wellies.'

In such austere surroundings, Jim Lawson asked James what luxuries, if any, he enjoys. James answered: 'Cigarettes and a wee dram.'

On his life at the bothy, James says: 'I fetch my water from a nearby river and often in winter it gets so cold I've got to break the ice to fill my bucket. My meals are cooked on an open fire using driftwood or peat, and I read by candle light.'

At the time of the interview, the bothy was furnished with two old chairs, a table and bed.

For most of the *Sunday Mail's* readers, the piece was simply a light-hearted look at the life of a man who had opted to turn his back on society and follow a different path. But for James' relatives it was a vital lifeline. It was confirmation he was still alive and well. Now they knew where he was, they were eager to meet up with him once again.

After contacting the *Sunday Mail*, arrangements were made for them to travel north. Sisters Winnie, Lilly and Lisbeth and nephew Andrew made the long journey from Dumbarton to Sutherland and booked into a bed and breakfast at Sheigra.

Plans were made for the family to meet in Kinlochbervie and, as he had done so often in the past, James washed himself in the stream adjacent to Strathchailleach and donned a clean shirt before embarking upon the long walk into town. This time, however, he would not only be picking up his pension and messages, he would be picking up on his past. According to Sallie Tyszko, he was apprehensive about the impending meeting.

'He was very nervous,' she said. 'He'd left his family years earlier and he was now in a place where people accepted him for who he was. Up here he was allowed to be who he was, free of anything in his past. I think he was worried they might have expected him to be the person they originally knew.

'I had to reassured him and the one thing I remember telling him is don't, whatever you do, get drunk before they arrive,' Sallie added.

On a dry, bright day, in the presence of Jim Lawson and a Press photographer, James was finally reunited with his family.

Photographs of the event show him smartly dressed in a dark jersey and long black overcoat and, as normal, he wore his flat cap.

'There were a few tears shed that day,' Jim recalled.

James reunited with his sisters Winnie, Lilly and Lisbeth – Andrew Smith

Winnie said: 'We met James in Kinlochbervie, at the hotel I think. It was brilliant, we still recognised him even after all that time. I knew I would. We talked and talked as if we had never been apart. That is the special thing about our family – we might not see someone for a long time but when we do meet up we talk as if we were together just yesterday.

'It was quite an emotional moment for all of us. We had not seen or heard from James for years so there was a lot to catch up on. I remember crying a few tears.

'James looked very healthy and happy. Life at the bothy obviously suited him. For the first time in years we now knew where he was and that he was still alive and enjoying his life,' she added.

The conversation centred on James' time at the bothy and how he survived in such extreme conditions. Little, if anything, was said about the years between him leaving home and arriving at

Strathchailleach. In return, his sisters updated him on what his brothers, sisters, nieces and nephews had been up to over the years.

The family brought with them gifts – thermal underwear, jerseys, a long coat and a bottle or two of whisky. James gratefully accepted all.

Although the three sisters remained in Kinlochbervie after the reunion, Andrew opted to accompany James home for a night at the bothy.

'We talked and drank long into the night,' he remembered. 'I thought the bothy was brilliant. My uncle had done paintings on the walls and he showed me a wee lochan nearby which he said he had stocked with trout. He told me how he tickled the trout to catch them.

'Inside there was furniture made from old orange boxes that he must have gathered on the beach. He had made the bothy very comfortable and a good fire kept us warm.

'I remember thinking how noisy it was out there. That surprised me. There were all sorts of noises, noises you don't hear in town. You could hear the running water from the wee burn behind the cottage and the wind and the birds. It was a great place to be.'

The following morning Andrew reluctantly bid farewell to his uncle and walked back to Kinlochbervie to rejoin his mother and aunts for the journey home. At no point did James contemplate leaving with them.

'The family came and went,' said Sallie Tyszko. 'It didn't change James. He didn't want to go back with them. In fact, at no point can I ever remember him ever expressing any desire to leave his bothy.'

Winnie, Lispeth and Lilly returned to Dumbarton, safe in the knowledge that their brother was happy and settled at Strathchailleach. The question that had hung in their minds for half a century had at last been answered.

For James, life at Strathchailleach continued as normal. His five minutes of fame brought news of his family and, despite his initial apprehension, he welcomed the opportunity to meet up with his sisters and share a glimpse of life at Strathchailleach with his nephew Andrew.

There was limited contact after the reunion. Niece Ella Connolly remembers sending Christmas cards. Like all of his mail, these were collected along with his pension when he visited Balchrick Post Office.

'I'd send Uncle James a card at Christmas,' she explained. 'In it I would write a few lines about what members of the family were doing, just to keep him up to date with what was happening.'

Although James did not return the favour, he did retain the cards and it was one of these cards that enabled friends to contact his family when he was taken seriously ill and admitted to hospital.

*****

9

In 1994 James was forced to relinquish his beloved bothy. Old age and ill health were taking their toll. The lengthy trek into Kinlochbervie for pension and provisions was becoming increasingly arduous while the long winter months were not kind to a man who was now well into his sixties.

Initial efforts to encourage James out of the wilderness and into the community all failed. The local authority offered him a council house in Kinlochbervie, but he stubbornly refused it. Offers of help from social services were bluntly rejected. Friends did what they could, but no one could convince James the time to leave Strathchailleach was fast approaching.

The last straw proved to be a lengthy bout of illness so serious it confined him to his bed for days. When he failed to appear as normal at Balchrick Post Office to collect his pension, concerned friends hiked to the bothy to find him in a distressed state.

James spent his final years in a caravan at Kinlochbervie's old harbour – James Carron

Unable to walk, he was airlifted from Strathchailleach to Raigmore Hospital in Inverness where he spent several days recuperating before being released.

It was clear to those who knew him that he was in no fit state to return to Strathchailleach, so friends found a vacant caravan in Kinlochbervie that belonged to a local salmon fisherman and they moved him in. It was basic by modern standards, but there was gas heating and lighting and running water. Located by the old Loch Clash pier, it was close to the village shop and harbour, although James continued to walk up to Balchrick Post Office to collect his pension. But he never went any further; he never headed back up the track to his former bothy home, no matter how tempting it may have been.

'One of his closest friends, Donald Morrison, helped move him out. He gathered up his belongings and moved them down to Kinlochbervie,' recalls Sallie Tyszko. 'James was very resilient and he looked after himself. He would never go to the doctor and nothing beat him. He was always incredibly hardy.

'In latter years, however, I think the tough conditions, particularly in the winter, were beginning to tell on him. He would get himself into trouble. This often happened in the winter and I think part of the reason for this was that he knew, if he was arrested, he would be taken to the police station at Rhiconich where he would get a warm bed and food.

'Usually it was not for anything too serious. He would break into holiday homes in the area and take tinned food. He didn't need it but in prison he was warm and got three good meals a day. There was some sympathy for him from local people who were not particularly happy about the growing number of holiday homes,' she added.

Ensconced in the village, he was a regular visitor to the harbour and took a keen interest in the activities of the fishermen and their boats. He often popped into Kinlochbervie Fishermen's Mission for a cup of tea or a hot meal and, to this day, a photograph of James, taken at the harbour, hangs on the wall within the cafeteria there.

Fish was always a central part of his diet at Strathchailleach and this remained the case in Kinlochbervie where harbour workers often handed him bags of surplus haddock or cod. Closer to the caravan, staff at the Spar grocery store took care of his pension, ensuring he didn't spend too much on alcohol. And he was never without visitors, keen to see how he was doing.

Drink still played a significant part in his life and it continued to bring trouble. Sallie believes James was unable to adapt to life in Kinlochbervie, having been so used to life in the great outdoors, with its fresh air and wide-open spaces. He was becoming increasingly frail.

'He was very reluctant to leave the bothy. He never settled in Kinlochbervie and his health was never the same,' she added.

This is a feeling echoed by his sister Winnie. 'He wasn't able to live at the bothy any longer but people say the move into Kinlochbervie was the beginning of the end for James. He went downhill from there. He was drinking heavily and he didn't have any privacy. And there were people who took advantage of him, plying him with drink and using his caravan as a drinking den.'

In his latter years, James regularly suffered from chest infections and in April 1999, when he was aged 75, he was admitted to Raigmore Hospital after falling seriously ill.

Friends made contact with his niece Ella Connolly and she and her husband George travelled north to visit him in hospital.

'I remember getting a call right out of the blue about James,' she said. 'A woman on the phone said she was trying to find his relatives. Apparently James had been taken ill and friends of his had searched his caravan to try and find some information about his family. In the end they found a Christmas card I had sent after the story appeared in the *Sunday Mail*. Through this the police had managed to get my name and number.'

Ella and George Connolly visited James in hospital. But four weeks later, on April 20, shortly after 2pm, he died from bronchopneumonia.

James McRory Smith – Howard Patrick

Sallie also visited him in hospital. 'In his final days he was talking a lot but no one could understand what he was saying,' she said. 'We asked him if we could bring him anything but he just said toast. We asked him if there was anything else and he just said he wanted toast and more toast.'

Just as James's life was ending, a new chapter was beginning at Strathchailleach. On April 1, 1999, five years after his reluctant departure from the cottage, a team of MBA volunteers arrived to renovate the bothy. They found the old house pretty much as James had left it.

With £3500 earmarked for the restoration, building supplies were airlifted in to avoid damage to the access path that crossed land now belonging to the John Muir Trust, a conservation charity, and work began in earnest.

The cottage itself was stable enough. However, the roof was completely renewed and guttering was installed along the front. The walls and chimney on the eastern gable were re-pointed and new windows and a new door were installed.

Rubbish was also removed from the site. There were empty whisky bottles and rusting beer cans dumped within the ruins of the outbuilding at the western end of the cottage along with mounds of old batteries. There were also old blankets and rugs, abandoned by James when they became too dirty or too threadbare for him to continue using.

The main room used by James was re-plastered but some of his artwork was retained and remains in the bothy to this day.

With James lying in the morgue at Raigmore Hospital, the task of organising his funeral fell to Sallie Tyszko. The service turned out to be every bit as unorthodox as James' life.

'When James died the hospital asked about relatives,' she explained. 'But at that point we had no idea where to find them. There was a funeral to arrange and I thought someone has go to do that. There was no one else so in the end it fell to me to contact the undertaker.

'We organised for James to be buried at Sheigra and arranged for a headstone to be made. All this time we were still trying to find his relatives so we could let them know what had happened and when the funeral would be taking place. Then a friend of mine found a letter with his sister's name and address and we were able to let them know.'

The undertaker brought James home and a request was made to the Church of Scotland to place his coffin in the kirk on the night before the service.

'Unfortunately they wouldn't let us do this,' Sallie continued. 'The church was set up for another service so in the end the undertaker just said he would take James home with him for the night. Only in the Highlands would that sort of think happen.'

The funeral took place on Saturday, April 24, four days after James' death. As the day dawned, there was still uncertainty over whether members of his family would arrive in time.

'The funeral service was due to start at one o'clock and the undertaker brought the coffin down to the church as planned. However, as one o'clock approached there was still no sign of his family. We had made contact with some of his relatives and they said they would come up. We waited for them outside the church but there was still no sign.

'At that point someone remembered his radio and how he had taken it with him everywhere he went. It seemed only fitting that he took it with him now. It was hurriedly found and, outside the church, we got the undertaker to open up the coffin and we placed it in, by his feet.

'We put the radio on, with the volume down low. There was a football commentary on and as the coffin was carried into the church a goal must have been scored and a loud 'hooray' filtered out of the coffin.'

With no sign of James' relatives and the service already half an hour late, there was no option but to start. Then, 15 minutes into the service, they arrived, casually dressed having had no time to change.

After picking James' nephew Andrew up from a hotel at Loch Awe where he was working at the time, the family travelled north. However, they underestimated the time it would take to reach Kinlochbervie.

James' sister Winnie said: 'We took a wrong turning along the way but eventually we reached the service. We were late arriving but we made it just in time. It was a lovely service and very well attended.'

After the service, the coffin was conveyed to the cemetery at Sheigra when it was lowered into the ground. Mourners, around 50 in all, then retired to the Kinlochbervie Hotel, where Bernard and Betty Heath laid on soup, sandwiches and a dram.

There remained the small matter of how the funeral would be paid for. Sallie set up a fund and a small grant was secured from the local council. James himself had left around £200, money held for him by the shop in Kinlochbervie. In addition, a collection was taken in the church. It was well supported, with many generous donations. But when Sallie returned to gather the money following the burial at Sheigra, she found it gone.

'When we went back to the church we found the dish was empty. We later discovered the church organist had banked it in the church account. They had it for six months before we got it back.'

It is somewhat ironic that the church ended up banking, albeit it mistakenly, money donated to pay for James' funeral as locals claim, on at least one occasion, he helped himself to the contents of the collection dish following Sunday service.

For almost a year, the grave in Sheigra cemetery remained unmarked. Then in March 2000 a headstone was erected.

The grave and headstone – James Carron

Carved by a local stonemason from a Caithness flagstone, the memorial features the image of a tern in flight created by Durness artist Nicky Powell. Below this there is the simple inscription: 'James McRory Smith, 1924-1999, Strathchailleach'.

Flowers were laid and a generous measure of Stewart's Cream of the Barley whisky was poured over the stone during a small ceremony attended by close friends.

As part of the renovation of Strathchailleach, a photograph of James McRory Smith was mounted on the wall of the small back room where he slept for so many years. Beneath the picture, there was a plaque.

Composed by Bernard Heath, the text read: 'Strathchailleach. This isolated house is though to be the last on mainland Scotland that was lived in as a permanent dwelling without services. No piped water, no sewerage services, electricity of gas. No postal services and no road, not even a proper path to the door.

'This was the adopted home of James McRory Smith who lived here as a recluse for thirty-two years. Better known as Sandy, he walked out for his pension to Balchrick Post Office and on to the shop, The London Stores beyond Kinlochbervie for his supplies, usually spending some time at the Garbet Hotel. His return route sometimes took him to the footbridge at Strathan where he sometimes overnighted, though he always described it as a cold house. This walk is about twenty-one miles in all and Sandy did this every week – winter and summer.

'Sandy had some other abilities as witnessed by his artwork on these walls. He was also known to be an astrologer. What kept him here for so long? The writer believes it was the close proximity of the finest naturally drying peat bank in the north. Sandy was rarely without a cosy fire.

'About 1996 he moved out to caravan accommodation in KLB. After a short illness he died on 20th April 1999 at Raigmore Hospital, Inverness, aged 75 years, and now lies at rest in the nearby cemetery at Sheigra. Over the recent years Sandy was, I believe, the living ghost seen by many in the bay at Sandwood. Now he is the real one.'

An intimation published in the Press & Journal newspaper on April 23, 1999, summed up James' life in fewer words. It described the recluse as a 'remarkable character in the area'. Whatever people thought of him – and there were many and varied views expressed over the years – there was no doubt he was indeed a remarkable character.

*****

Acknowledgements

A great deal of research has gone into the production of this book and the author is deeply indebted to many people for their willing and enthusiastic help, help without which it could not have been completed. To all those who so freely contributed of their time and knowledge, I would like to offer my heartfelt thanks. Particular gratitude must go to Sallie Tyszko and to the family of James McRory Smith who were so generous with their time, tea and biscuits, particularly Winnie Kilpatrick, Andrew Smith, Elizabeth Smith and Ella Connelly.

Thanks also go to Barry Abbot, Alistair Currie, Matt Dawson, Bridget Graham, Bernard Heath, John Mackay, Norman Morrison, Steve Moss, Rod Shepherd, John Slater, Bert Wallace, and Francis and Janet Whittington for their recollections and to Howard Patrick for his excellent photographs.

I must also thank journalist Jim Lawson and the staff of the Daily Record & Sunday Mail Ltd archive; Duncan Smith, librarian at Aberdeen Journals Ltd; Donald MacLeod, editor of Am Bratach; Thomas B. Smyth, archivist at the Black Watch Museum in Perth; the staff of both Inverness Library and Brora Library; the staff of the National Library of Scotland in Edinburgh; the staff of New Register House, Edinburgh; and the staff of The National Archives of Scotland in Edinburgh.

Other sources consulted include the John Muir Trust Journal, January 2005; Mountain Bothies Association Journal, 1980 and 1981; Mountain Bothies Association Newsletter, various; Northern Times; Press & Journal; Sunday Mail; Census Records for the Parish of Eddrachillis; The Report of the Survey of the Parishes of Assynt and Eddrachillis by AW Adam and I Rankin (1964); A Survey of Shelters in Remote Mountain Areas of the Scottish Highlands by Ian Mackenzie, Perth; Highways & Byways in the West Highlands by Seton Gordon (1935); Kinlochbervie by Alexander Macrae (The Highland Christian Literature Society, Tongue); Mountain Bothies Association bothy log book, Strathchailleach; The Third Statistical Account of Scotland, The County of Sutherland, edited by John S.

Smith (Scottish Academic Press, Edinburgh, 1988); and various Ordnance Survey maps published in 1873, 1878, 1908 and 1927/28.

To all those mentioned I must express once again my thanks. I am aware there are gaps in the story, ones that have to date been impossible to fill. However, I would be delighted to hear from anyone who can add anything further to the remarkable life story of James McRory Smith.

*****

Printed in Germany
by Amazon Distribution
GmbH, Leipzig